ON TARGET

a design and manage target cost procurement system

ON TARGET
a design and manage target cost procurement system

DAVID TRENCH

Thomas Telford, London

Published by Thomas Telford Ltd, Thomas Telford House, 1 Heron Quay, London E14 4JD

First published 1991

A CIP catalogue record for this book is available from the British Library.

ISBN: 0 7277 1646 8

Typeset in Great Britain by RhysJones Consultants, Halley House, 49 Burney Street, Greenwich, London

Printed and bound in Great Britain by Butler & Tanner Ltd, Frome and London

Acknowledgements

There are a number of business colleagues both in client, fellow professional organisations and Trench Farrow & Partners who have assisted in the writing of this book whom I would like to thank; particularly Robert Heskett of Land Securities PLC and Sir Michael Palmer, previously with Credit Lyonnais who as clients backed our development of the system and paid the legal costs of drafting contracts; Peter Barber of Clifford Chance (now at Freshfields) for pioneering the first contract; Martin Bridgewater of Nabarro Nathanson for providing a plain English guide to the contracts and further refinements of Peter's work; and David Williams of How Design & Management Limited whose own work at Reading University on the same theme gave me the trade contractor's viewpoint.

I would also like to thank Alan Moore whose dissertation written for the Project Management degree course at Reading University provided valuable information and assistance; Derek Gillingham of Haden Young who provided me with two thoughtful papers which he had written and some of his ideas have been included; Ron Denny who read and commented on the manuscript; my wife Rita for putting up with me being attached to my tape recorder by the swimming pool for the whole of last summer's holiday and Roderick Rhys Jones who edited the manuscript.

David Trench
1 January 1991

Preface

Many developers, professionals and contractors working in the construction industry are conscious of their responsibility to implement constructive change. New technology, forms of building structures, off-site engineering and fabrication have changed the nature of design and construction. Some of these developments have come from within the industry, others have come from the aerospace, automotive and electronic industries. Where the new technologies of CAD/CAM have become firmly established, the traditional skills of design and construction based on a sound knowledge of masonry and carpentry are giving way to these new technologies. The separate skills of pure design and contract management have been recognised. It is time to challenge the procurement systems of the 19th Century which are underpinned by many of the standard building contracts currently being offered to the industry's clients as the appropriate way to commission construction work. It is time to break down the present sterile interface between designer and contractor so that their knowledge and experience combine to benefit the project.

A major feature of the system of procurement advocated in this manual is that it encourages a different way of working. It responds to the emerging need for the client, system designer and manufacturer to come together in a mood of collaboration and support to find the most appropriate solution to a particular design need. The term 'sub-consultant' used in the text in no way implies a reduction in the status of a consultant. It is a method of differentiating between the roles of the consultants involved in a project before and after the contract for construction has been let. Construction, being a highly personalised process, requires team working. If real synergy can be realised from all members of the team during and prior to construction whilst providing developers with good value for money then a new dawn is heralded for all those involved in the building and development process.

Contents

Summary

This manual describes a new system of target cost building procurement whereby:

- [ ] a more equitable balance is set between employer's risk and contractor's risk than by other common procurement systems,
- [ ] the quality of design is improved because trade contractors contribute to the design philosophy and detailing early in the project and perhaps before the main contractor is appointed,
- [ ] the contractor appointed to manage the final design and work of the sub-contractors has an incentive to complete the project to an agreed target cost.

Savings or overruns, within a band, are shared with the employer according to an agreed formula which reflects market conditions and the level of risk perceived by the contractors. In addition the employer can obtain a guaranteed maximum price so that it is known before building begins what the ceiling of his construction costs will be.

This system of procurement has been used successfully by the author. Experience shows that contractors, designers and employers work more easily together using this system than on many conventionally procured projects where the balance of risk has been less fair, and conflict more likely.

This manual explains the philosophy behind the system and then describes each of the eight stages in the system in detail. Appendices 1-3 contain examples or explanatory memoranda of the three key contracts that are required to implement the system.

The system does not provide a panacea for all the problems of late, over budget, or acrimonious contracts. It is best suited to contracts where there are risks which are unlikely to be borne by contractors at a reasonable premium, where time is of the essence and construction needs to progress before design is completed. It will suit large, complex or innovative projects.

Those who complete the reading of this document might think that the system described is more complicated and time consuming in its detail than the traditional systems accepted for so many years by building owners in general. In fact it is not. The truth is that the stages of traditional contracting have seldom been analysed in similar depth nor committed to paper in a logical manner.

It is hoped that this manual will make some contribution to the continuing debate on improving the contractual methods by which we construct our buildings.

A new approach to building procurement

RISK MANAGEMENT

Risk is inherent in all construction projects. The management of risk is fundamental to the success of a project. Developers who typically allow 20 per cent profit margins on their cost appraisals cannot expect to transfer the majority of construction risks to contractors working on margins of between 2.5 per cent and five per cent. Developers can make a greater or lesser return on their investment depending on property market conditions. Contractors, on the other hand, can gain nothing from changes in the market. Once they have priced a contract the percentage profit margin invariably diminishes as problems materialise. It is unlikely that developers will be successful in transferring the majority of risk to contractors in the foreseeable future without paying for it. There are probably too many main contractors in the UK, compared with other European countries, and the intense competition for survival means that margins for main contractors are likely to remain low for the next decade.

The largest single cause of cost overruns on projects is when control of the programme is lost and the contract period is exceeded. NEDO's most recent figures on commercial buildings (*NEDO Faster Building for Commerce, Construction Industry Sector Group*, published by NEDO, HMSO 1988) show that a third of 260 projects overran their contract programme. Furthermore the larger the project the greater the likelihood of programme overruns. The author has failed to find a commercial project over £50m which was completed to its initial contract completion date in London during the 1985-90 boom. Many of them overran by as much as 40 per cent. The issue of time and therefore cost overruns can be resolved to a great extent by managing risk more assiduously.

The response to risk by all parties involved in the construction process can be considered in terms of:

- ☐ Avoidance.
- ☐ Reduction.
- ☐ Transfer.
- ☐ Retention.
- ☐ Insurance.

Anybody developing a procurement system should analyse carefully the most likely attitude and response of each party to the various categories of risk to which each is exposed. Risks wrongly placed may have such serious consequences as to endanger the viability of a project.

Most standard forms of contract have their origins in the 19th Century when main contractors carried out almost all the work themselves. This system prevailed up to two decades ago, main contractors still carrying out about 45 per cent of the works directly. This proportion of the works normally consisted of those structural elements of the project which suffer the vagaries of construction risks such as weather, labour disputes and ground risks. Now main contractors often carry out less than 20 per cent of the works with the rest sub-contracted to trade and specialist contractors. The contracts now being used do not reflect these changes. Of particular concern is the transference of risk from the main contractor to a less sophisticated trade contract market. Many firms of trade contractors are ill equipped and not geared to cope with the adverse effect of risk. The system of procurement outlined later in this book recognises that trade contractors carry out at least 80 per cent value of the works on a typical project and that the interrelationships between trade contractors who have no contractual links with each other are vital to the efficiency and successful outcome of the whole project.

Each risk has a cost which must ultimately be borne by the employers of an industry if it is to remain profitable and thus survive. The party best able to control the circumstances that could lead to loss will price the risk of that loss the lowest. Therefore to reduce the cost to the employer that party should be allocated the risk. The principal aim of a successful procurement system is to ensure that risks are managed efficiently to best protect the project as a whole and not to protect the individual party often at the project's expense. This, of course, includes the employer who will always bear some risk, albeit transferred to outside parties such as insurance companies. However, no matter how much care and attention is paid to allocating the risks to the most relevant party, risk will not, by its nature, be removed.

The most common way of dealing with residual risk is for each party to allocate an overall contingency sum out of which all residual risks are paid. Any procurement system should give careful thought to this allocation and control of contingencies. The present arbitrary system of adding an overall percentage to the total anticipated capital expenditure is crude and unsatisfactory, particularly on competitively tendered projects.

The more risk the employer transfers to other parties, the more he must expect to pay for this privilege. Thus the employer should ensure that risk is wisely transferred as it is in its own best financial interests.

The following questions should be answered when allocating risk:

☐ Which party can best control or influence the events that might lead to loss?

☐ Which party can best manage the events relating to loss, if it occurs?

☐ Is it preferable for the employer to retain some involvement in the management of the risk?

☐ Is the premium likely to be charged for transferring the risk reasonable?

☐ Can the party to whom the risk is transferred sustain the consequences if loss occurs?

☐ Will transfer of risk result in other risks of a different nature being transferred back to the employer so as to defeat the employer's risk management strategy?

☐ Will the transfer of risk create resentment that could have a detrimental effect on the project?

An indication of the financial benefit to employers prepared to adopt more flexible attitudes to forms of contract was given in the *New York Business Round Table Report: Contractual arrangements in the US construction industry* (October 1982). This report suggested that five per cent of project costs may be saved by choosing the most appropriate form of contract. This is probably an under-estimate of the savings that could be made in the UK.

Work completed under a construction contract is paid for in two ways; either as fixed-price, lump-sum items (price-based contracts) or as cost-reimbursable items (cost-based contracts). Fixed-price items are paid for on the basis of prices tendered by a contractor before it starts work. These tender prices include an allowance for overhead, risk and profit which normally reflects the contractor's work load and the market situation. Cost-reimbursable items are paid for on the basis of the actual cost incurred by the contractor as it completes the work. An additional sum is paid to cover profit and any overheads which are not defined as reimbursable in the contract. Table 1 expresses the risk implication in different types of contract.

Price-based contracts require the contractor to carry a greater proportion of risks than cost-reimbursable contracts. The contractor will estimate the risk it is carrying and reflect this in its prices, or rates in the form of hidden contingencies. Those risks such as unforeseen ground conditions which entitle the contractor to claim additional payment through the contract will be disregarded by the contractor and are borne by the employer. However, the way in which claims are made and adjudicated make the level of additional payment little more than a gamble for the contractor and the employer. The higher the uncertainty, the greater chance of that gamble reaching the point where its outcome spells disaster for a project.

On the other hand cost-based contracts require the employer to carry the majority of, if not all, the risks. The employer will pay the actual costs of dealing with any unforeseen occurrences. The cost will be based on the contractor's accounts which are open for inspection. However, because the contractor is assured of its costs and profit (unless found negligent) there is no incentive for the contractor to control costs or manage risks.

Between the two extremes of fixed-price lump-sum contracts on the one hand and cost-reimbursable contracts on the other, are a wide variety of contracts which include both methods of payment. The labelling of the contract type very much depends upon which mechanism predominates at main contractor level. It can be seen from Figure 1 that as the contract includes more fixed-price lump-sum elements, the employer's risk declines and the contractor's rises. Similarly as the contract includes a greater proportion of cost-reimbursable elements the employer's risk rises and the contractor's risk declines.

There are a number of other important characteristics of these two types of contract. Employers have less flexibility to change their requirements with a fixed-price contract. Any changes are the cause of contractor's claims and these are difficult to adjudicate without a knowledge of the contractor's rates which are normally confidential. Employers have more flexibility if the contract includes more cost-reimbursable elements.

Fixed-price contracts are easier for the employer to manage than cost-reimbursable contracts, see Figure 2. As more cost-reimbursable

Table 1: Risk implications of different types of contract

Characteristic	PRICE-BASED		COST-BASED	
	JCT No Bill of Quantities Lump-Sum	Bill of Quantities Unit Price	Target Cost	Cost-Reimbursable
Financial objectives of client and contractor	Different but reasonably independent. Quality of tender information vital	Different and potential conflict	Considerable harmony. Reduction of actual cost is a common objective if cost remains in the incentive region	Both based on actual cost but potentially in conflict as risks are controlled by contractor but paid for by employer
Flexibility for design change	Very limited	Some	Extensive	Unlimited
Evaluation of change by client	Little or no information available from tender	Mainly based on tendered prices and rates	Target adjustment based on actual costs & utilisation of resources or target rates available	Unnecessary for contractual purposes. Actual costs paid.
Design/construction overlap: early start to construction	Impracticable and risky to employer	Feasible but relatively limited	Considerable opportunity	Construction may be started when first design package is available
Contractor's involvement in design of permanent works	Excluded	Usually excluded	Contractor encouraged to contribute ideas for reducing actual cost	Contractor may be appointed for design input prior to construction
Client involvement in construction management	Excluded	Retrospective	Recommended through joint planning	Should be active
Payment for risks	Undisclosed contingency in contractor's tender	Undisclosed contingency in contractor's tender plus claims	Payment of actual cost of dealing with risk. Target adjusted accordingly	Payment of actual cost
Claims resolution	Very difficult – no basis for evaluation	Difficult – client has no knowledge of actual cost or hidden contingency	Potentially easy – based on actual costs or target costs. Mechanism needs careful drafting	Unnecessary except for fee adjustment – usually relatively easy
Knowledge of final price at tender (excluding inflation)	Known – however, price usually increased by variations and claims	Uncertain – tender price usually increased by variations and claims	Uncertain – tender target cost usually increased by variations but effective joint management and efficient working can reduce final payment to below target cost	Unknown

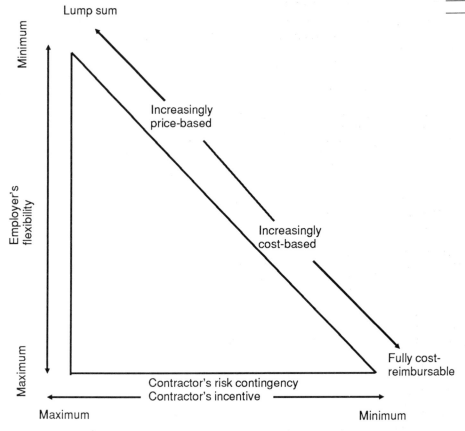

Figure 1: Basic characteristics of various types of construction contract

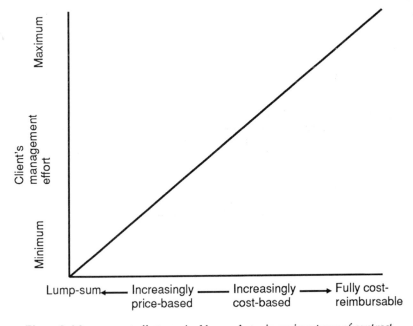

Figure 2: Management effort required by employer in various types of contract

elements are built into the contract the employer becomes more and more involved with the auditing and management of the contract – mostly to agree additional expenditure and to protect its interests.

The aim of the procurement system described in this manual is to introduce financial incentives to a cost-based contract which encourage the contractor to control the cost of coping with unforeseen circumstances.

FIXED-PRICE STANDARD FORMS OF CONTRACT

Fixed-price contracts are used for approximately 85 per cent of all building contracts let in the UK. This figure includes the price-based contracts which comprise the sub-contract packages which are part of management contracts. The 85 per cent reflects the comfort level employers require to convince themselves that prices reflect value for money in the competitive market place.

Price-based contracts include one or more of the following standard features:

☐ Lump-sum fixed-price.
☐ Bills of quantities or schedule of rates.
☐ Remeasurement.
☐ Turnkey.

Their use is probably inappropriate in the following circumstances:

☐ Where design needs to be comprehensively developed after tenders have been submitted.
☐ When the work to be contracted is innovative or pioneering.

The most commonly used standard forms of price-based contracts in the building industry belong to the JCT family. JCT standard forms of contract are mostly complex and often contentious. The Joint Contracts Tribunal responsible for their production now has 32 members representing 12 different industry associations and institutions plus two observers representing the CBI. The majority of the organisations represented are not party to the agreement between clients and contractors. Only two client organisations are represented, namely local authorities and the British Property Federation. Each contract must be unanimously accepted by the 12 member organisations each looking to cover their own interests. As a result these contracts make no effort to encourage proper risk management or reward efficient working. In addition they do nothing to reduce the incidence of disputes and the amount of money under dispute.

They do however have some advantages:

☐ They are well understood by the industry and do not rely on lawyers to point out risk.
☐ There is an established body of case law associated with them.
☐ They are deemed to be fair and equitable to both parties by the courts.
☐ They do not require costly drafting.

However, the value of these advantages is often exaggerated, particularly by professional quantity surveyors and estimators who feel comfortable with the standard forms and who have developed their own sophisticated methods of exploiting inadequacies. Furthermore, as a result of the arrangements developed under these standard contracts, the employer and the design team have become distanced from valuation and payment procedures.

In economic downturns contractors are inclined to tender low and claim high. Survival is paramount and the inefficient can recoup their losses by systematic exploitation of the clauses appertaining to extensions of time and loss and expense claims on the back of failures of the employer's agents to provide adequate information at the right time. Many standard forms are notoriously adversarial and the valuable resources of the contractor, professional quantity surveyors, designers and even the employer can be tied up in dealing with claims and counter claims. At worst the building itself becomes a byproduct of this activity rather than the 'raison d'être'.

COST-BASED BESPOKE CONTRACTS

Standard forms of contract are less appropriate for large, complex or costly projects particularly those with critical completion deadlines or innovative design features. Where time is of the essence and design needs to overlap the construction period, a cost-based contract can provide an appropriate solution. Where the employer wishes the contractor to bear part of the risk in a cost-based contract then consideration should be given to a bespoke contract to meet the requirements of the employer's risk management strategy. However, one contract, *JCT 87 Management Form* and its *Pro Forma Works Contract*, can be used where the employer wishes to shoulder all construction risk with the singular exception of contractor negligence. It has its critics and like almost all forms of management contract it is untested in the courts. The important point about this contract however, is that all trade contractors who actually undertake the work are appointed by the management contractor. The management contractor's liability for default is limited to what it can recover from the works sub-contractors. There is no cost ceiling for the employer. The performance of the management contractor relies on how important it views retaining a good reputation in the market place. There is little other incentive to perform well, manage risks or save money.

At the moment there is no real alternative to engaging a firm of lawyers specialising in construction law to write a bespoke contract. Unfortunately standard forms of contract are frequently amended by employers, contractors and professional quantity surveyors seeking to move the risk line. The resultant conditions however may be biased and might, if tested, fall foul of the *Unfair Contract Terms Act 1977*. Furthermore the knock-on effect of altering one clause can cause other clauses to fail when tested in the courts or by arbitration.

ADVANTAGES OF BESPOKE CONTRACTS
The advantages of a bespoke contract are:

- ☐ The employer benefits from a tailored, clearer allocation of the risks and responsibilities.
- ☐ Contracts can be made simpler, easier to administer and be a genuine tool to assist management of the works.
- ☐ A tailor-made building contract is a relatively small portion of the cost of a large project.
- ☐ Bespoke contracts can take account of case law related to standard forms.

- ☐ If a contract is drafted by the employer in conjunction with contractors who have an opportunity to comment in advance of bidding, then the extent to which the resultant contract might be construed as 'contra proferentem' would be minimised.

- ☐ Selection procedures for the contractor would include discussion on the allocation of risk and the conditions of contract.

- ☐ The contract can include incentives for the contractor to reduce costs and schedule the project for timely completion.

- ☐ Faster methods of dispute resolution can be introduced which reduce unnecessary expense and delay.

FIXED-PRICE DESIGN-BUILD CONTRACTS

In December 1983 the British Property Federation, BPF, published *The BPF System for building design and construction.* This was a method of project procurement intended to reduce claims and disputes. The design is carried sufficiently far so that on the basis of drawings and the detailed specification, tenderers can give sensible, competitive prices for completing the design and carrying out the construction. The amount of design to be carried out by the contractor will vary very considerably. For a simple shed it is probably sufficient to give tenderers the drawings produced for detailed planning permission together with a very detailed specification. For a complicated building, much more needs to be designed and there is far less room for contractor input. In all cases, however, the contractor becomes responsible for any design which he carries out. This system gives the contractor more control over the management of the contract and reduces the employer's risk. Unfortunately *The BPF System* has not achieved its aims of rewarding those contractors that are efficient and therefore many contractors shy away from this form of high risk tendering. It is this issue that the procurement system described here addresses.

The author's firm Trench Farrow was appointed client's representative on three very different projects on which *The BPF System* was used:

- ☐ £57m high class commercial office block in central London.
- ☐ £16m comprehensive refurbishment of a 1960 London office block.
- ☐ £6m mixed offices and shopping scheme retaining nine listed buildings in Kent.

However, the *BPF/ACA Contract,* itself developed for use with *The BPF System,* was not used principally because of the largely hostile reception by the contracting industry at its launch. Instead *JCT 81 with Contractor Design* was used with 32 amendments which brought it largely into line with the *BPF/ACA Contract.* Furthermore the contractor was asked to adopt the design (take responsibility for the design embodied in the employer's requirements). Whilst being onerous to the contractors, this avoided splitting responsibility for design and removed a number of grey areas on the question of what constituted design development and what constituted a change in the employer's requirements. The Joint Contracts Tribunal has now amended *JCT 81* so that with all the amendments and the supplement it closely accords with *The BPF System.*

The benefits of operating The BPF System were similar on all three contracts:

- All projects kept fairly closely to schedule.
- All projects were completed within the tender price plus two per cent contingency (excluding certain employer's enhancements added as variation orders).
- All projects produced a harmonious relationship between the employer and the contractor. Attitudes were very constructive.
- Because of the perceived high risk, all projects were allocated particularly high calibre construction teams which performed very efficiently. A resident construction board director was allocated to one major scheme which reflects the risk perceived from the contractor's viewpoint.
- The resolution of design issues was seldom a problem. The contractor had a major input into such resolution and admitted to learning much about design.
- Relationships between main contractor and sub-contractor were good and sub-contractors of proven track record were often chosen in preference to those tendering the lowest price.
- The quality of work was better than on many traditional contracts yet the employer's supervision was substantially less than one would expect to see on traditionally managed projects.
- The contractors took a long term view on liability for defects and went some way to reassuring themselves on design issues such as waterproofing details.
- The design teams responded to making construction easier by altering the detail of design without lowering the specification.
- Variations were priced as the project progressed and the final account was settled within a short time from completion.
- Towards the end of the design period the design team preparing the employer's requirements, worked around the clock to produce a complete design that the contractor could not downgrade. The finality of not being allowed to tinker with designs after the project was priced by the contractor spurred the design team to meet deadlines. Records indicate that approximately one hour of design resource was needed to produce £500 (1988) of construction value of work at the required quality. The resultant tender documents were more comprehensive than those prepared for most traditional contracts. So from the start on-site the project was fully defined. The concern that the contractor could earn the design consultants a bad name proved to be a very effective weapon in determining quality of the design consultants' output. It also brought out the employer's decisions and choices early in the design process.
- Because the design consultants were working for the contractor, paperwork in respect of communication and information was significantly reduced.
- Valuations and payment procedures were simple and the professional quantity surveyor's work load was front loaded in administering the tender and preparing much of the documentation. The construction

period and settlement of final accounts were substantially less demanding in resources.

☐ The design consultants learned far more about the detail of costs and practicalities of their design than they would under a conventional system.

DISADVANTAGES OF THE BPF SYSTEM (Author's observations)

The disadvantages of operating The BPF System on the three contracts were:

☐ Despite the contractors performing efficiently they all lost money. On all three projects the second lowest tender price was most accurate. It does not auger well in the long term for contractors to associate a particular procurement system with loss making projects.

☐ The contractors underestimated the hidden costs of design development. Additional material and labour costs not obvious to estimators measuring off drawings that appear to be well developed can quite easily add five per cent to the basic pricing.

☐ Operating in a rapidly inflating sub-contractor market, the main contractor on one of the projects had the dilemma of whether to place orders quickly on incomplete information or to lose time in developing complete designs. Either way he lost.

☐ Many sub-contractors were unwilling to accept the main contractor's terms and conditions of contract on a back-to-back basis. This particularly applied to the level of liquidated and ascertained damages and the principle of adopting the consultants' designs to the employer's requirements. This left the main contractor exposed.

☐ The employer's requirements were so advanced in detail in order to guarantee the quality of the end product that there was little opportunity for the contractor to make cost savings in the design to compensate for additional costs arising from adverse risks. Thus from the beginning the contractor was more likely to lose than gain money from the effects of unforeseen circumstances.

☐ *The BPF System* was launched in 1983 when the building industry was in recession. In the 1985-89 boom that followed it became apparent that many contractors would not bid low prices for large or complex design-build projects when such high risks were being assigned to them.

Some take the view that when tenderers and contractors are carefully briefed on the content of the BPF/ACA form of contract and on the different allocation of risks, and have experience of the system, they perform well and make normal profits. Certainly, one major contractor has worked with *The BPF System* on a number of occasions and is happy to go on doing so. The benefits of *The BPF System* have been impressive and it should not be discarded because contractors have initially failed to make profits using this system. This is principally because contractors consistently under-estimate the cost of managing and carrying out the completion of design. In developing the target cost system, described here, the author has re-examined *The BPF System* and altered it to reduce the amount of risk incurred by the contractor so that the efficient contractor makes a profit.

Under a target cost contract the actual cost of completing the work is evaluated and compared with an estimate or target cost of the work and the differences within a cost band are shared between employer and contractor.

Of course target cost contracts are not the only way of contracting. However the author and others have used this method of procurement successfully – testing largely unchartered UK water. This manual sets out in detail a target cost procurement method which should prove useful in the armoury of anyone contemplating development and weighing up which contract will suit a given situation.

A target cost contract can best be applied:

- ☐ Where there are large risk elements involved which the construction industry is unlikely to shoulder at a reasonable price.
- ☐ Where preconstruction advice is an essential ingredient.
- ☐ Where there is a need to commence construction activities before design is completed.
- ☐ Where time is of the essence.
- ☐ Where the project is very complex, very large or innovative.
- ☐ Where areas of uncertainty exist.

ADVANTAGES OF TARGET COST CONTRACTS

The advantages of a target cost contract are that it:

- ☐ Gives the contractor incentive to reduce costs to the the employer's benefit.
- ☐ Attracts the right team.
- ☐ Allows for preconstruction planning and advice to be available during the development of design.
- ☐ Is less adversarial than traditional forms.
- ☐ Will allow fast track by overlapping of final design and construction.
- ☐ Is easy to administer.
- ☐ Places risks with the party best able to deal with them.
- ☐ Allows resources to be controlled with maximum economy.
- ☐ Forces through early cost/design decisions.
- ☐ Allows the employer direct access to trade contractors and suppliers, if he so wishes.
- ☐ Produces greater cost certainty.
- ☐ Promotes a more circumspect and enquiring attitude to design within the contractor's organisation and encourages value engineering to the employer's benefit.

DISADVANTAGES OF TARGET COST CONTRACTS

The only real disadvantage of target cost contracts is that they are difficult to use successfully on contracts where many changes are expected because they do not have the flexibility.

SPECIALIST COMPONENT AND SYSTEMS DESIGN

Most current forms of contract were developed at a time when architects, with a sound knowledge of carpentry and masonry, detailed almost all elements of a building. These detailed plans were, and still are, used for taking off full bills of quantities, pricing, and construction.

The professionals were reimbursed fees on 'quantum meruit' or percentages of construction value and contractors were reimbursed on a fixed-price lump-sum tender. Thus the design and building processes were separate functions. This separation of function replaced an earlier process whereby the master builder took responsibility for both the detailed design and construction.

Today most components are manufactured on a truly international basis. Many features are designed by manufacturers rather than architects and components have become more technically sophisticated. It has therefore become increasingly important to find a way of incorporating the manufacturer's and trade contractor's design knowledge into the design process of the project. The conundrum is how to do this using standard forms of contract.

Until the procurement process is completed by the contractor and orders are placed with trade contractors many features of the design are incomplete. The resolution of interface problems between one trade contractor's design and another can only take place at a very late stage in the contract, long after all parties are committed to a price. Thus practically all systems of traditional contracting, in which the main contractor does not have design responsibility, are doomed to difficulties or at worst failure. It is impossible for consultants to produce a complete set of tender drawings which will not be subject to radical alteration of various aspects when trade contractors are appointed during construction. On those small projects where the outcome has been successful, it has been despite the system. Inefficiency costs on such projects are small and contractors have not felt it worthwhile to revert to the contract for reimbursement of losses or shortfall in anticipated profit.

The most common cause of claims is 'late or incomplete information' which affects the procurement and construction process resulting in requests for extensions of time. Standard forms of contract place the architect in the role of contract administrator. He/she is effectively judge and jury in the resolution of claims often reflecting on the efficiency of his/her own practice. Small wonder adversarial behaviour became commonplace. The ever increasing reliance on trade contractor drawings and information to determine the last parts of the design jigsaw exacerbate the problem of failure to issue adequate information in a timely fashion.

Figure 3 subjectively illustrates the normal period of total design in the context of construction activity. Design in this case means from concept to working drawings on, say, a £30 million project. *JCT 80* with domestic sub-contractors demonstrates the danger of specialist design taking place after a fixed tender price is agreed. *JCT 80* with nominated sub-contractors and prime cost sums means that the employer takes on certain responsibilities for the sub-contractor's performance, particularly in respect of delay and solvency. Conventional management contracting and its packaging and procurement process allows specialist design to take place after the estimated prime cost has been agreed and long after work has started on site. The system advocated by the author ensures that the principal trade contractor specialist design is undertaken up front and before the target cost is agreed. Furthermore, this is without a severe premium to the earliest start to construction.

A successful procurement system should incorporate the following criteria:

- ☐ Bring the principal trade contractors' designers aboard early in design development and prior to the employer's and main contractor's final commitments on price. The nominated sub-contractor procedure associated with *JCT 63* and *JCT 80* was designed to do this. However, under such circumstances the employer is liable for performance of such nominations. This has led to confused arrangements whereby the employer persuades the main contractor to adopt his preferred choice of sub-contractor thereby transferring liability for the associated risks. The legality of this practice is suspect.
- ☐ Recognise that the procurement process of selecting trade contractors should investigate design options involving research and development and value engineering which takes time.
- ☐ Appreciate that the quality in the design of interface between trade contractor packages is as important as the quality of contractor workmanship.
- ☐ Ensure that principal design consultants have direct access to trade contractors during the early stages of design development and do not have to work through a third party main contractor acting as a conduit or post box.
- ☐ Be aware that prices based on approved trade contractor drawings and specification will have a greater chance of being upheld than prices based on consultants' information.
- ☐ Understand that factory production schedules and capacities (including specialist trade contractor design office staff) are a finite resource and require planning and phasing to suit both the commercial aims of the specialist and the project.
- ☐ Aim to provide clients with competitive prices. The consultants should carry the trade contractor packages to the stage where it is possible for, say, three trade contractors to give sensible competitive prices for completing the design and carrying out the construction. There may, however, be some projects where the particular designers have difficulty carrying the design to this stage. It is then necessary to appoint a specialist trade contractor as part of the design team. Some way then has to be found of ensuring that the designing trade contractor gives a competitive price for the construction work which it subsequently carries out.

Given that procurement has become inextricably linked with component design and that craft has given way to technology, it is suggested that the contractor carrying out the management function of site assembly should also manage any residual design in the construction stage and bear the responsibilities that go with it. If we turn to other industries that have moved from craft to technology, there are parallels. In shipbuilding the naval architect and shipwright have merged to offer a single source of responsibility under large enterprises such as Harland and Wolff, Vickers and Vosper Thorneycroft. Within the building industry the mechanical and electrical industry has always offered design co-ordination as a normal service within construction sub-contracts simply because until components are placed on order and plant is chosen the design cannot be completed.

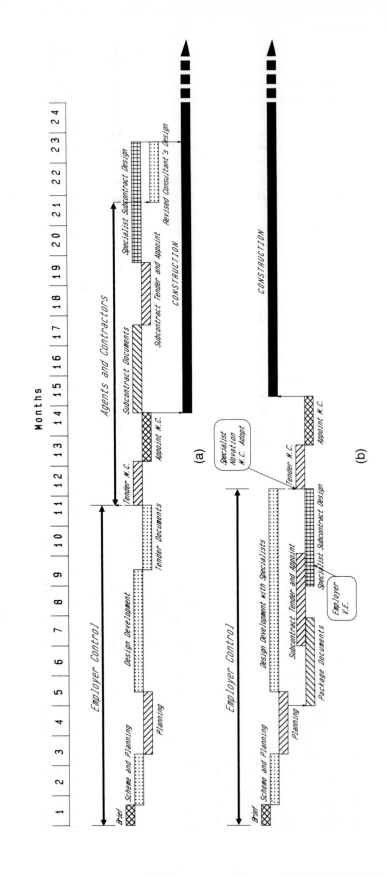

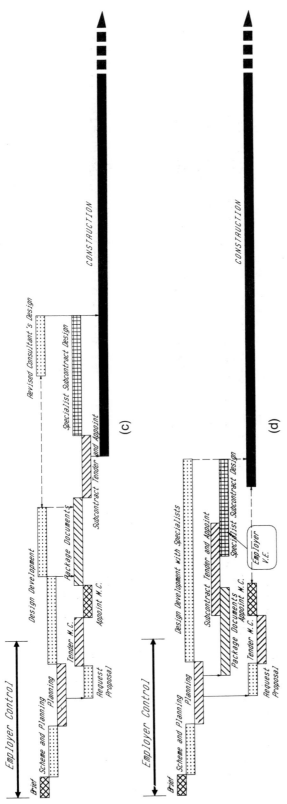

Figure 3: Periods of design and construction: (a) fixed price tendered JCT 80 contract with nominated sub-contractors; (b) fixed price tendered JCT 80 contract with domestic sub-contractors; (c) management contract JCT 87 with specialist design following procurement; (d) target cost design and manage contract with specialist design prior to agreement on d&m contractor and target cost

Would you put out to tender the manufacture of a car or aeroplane without having chosen an engine?

EMPLOYER FLEXIBILITY AND VARIATIONS

Variations at any stage during planning, procurement and construction are usually far more disruptive than they first appear. The notion that equipped with a JCT contract and a full bill of quantities you could start building a hospital and change its design to a prison and still retain full control of the price, using bills of quantities, is a dangerous illusion. It is an illusion that encourages designers and employers to change their mind or postpone decisions. The contractor, finding itself in a contractual pricing strait-jacket, uses doubtful claims as a means of recouping actual costs of variable work and this leads to sour relationships and, in the extreme, the physical collapse of projects.

There has also been a deliberate tendency by the employer, and the contractor's surveyors, to leave the pricing of variations until after the work has been done or until the end of the job. This leaves little incentive to execute the variation efficiently and leaves the main contractor and trade contractors to carry out the work as an act of blind faith that they will be reimbursed fairly.

Arguments ensue months after the work is finished as to whether daywork sheets are valid or whether the work should be valued under the contract. Cost reports of a project become a complete guessing game, in extreme cases, with sections of the report described as variations instructed but not priced, anticipated variations and possible variations under review. It all comes to a head at final account stage and is often the subject of a Dutch auction.

Variations are of course, almost always necessary. They take account of changes in legislation, technology and markets during the life of the project. At worst this can mean whole sections of radical redesign and at best subtle but disruptive alterations often colloquially referred to as 'fine tuning'.

Procurement systems need to incorporate some flexibility to cope with changes in the employer's requirements.

It is self-evident that the following information should be provided before work starts on a variation:

☐ Overall price.
☐ Changes in resource, method of work, timing and sequence of proposal.
☐ Quantity involved.
☐ Length of time involved including design and procurement.

However, greater efficiency and fairness could be achieved if the following concepts were incorporated in procurement systems:

☐ Ground rules for the pricing of variations incorporated in tender documentation albeit in the form of provisional sums or schedule of rates. The contractors are then able to price attendance, profit and programming consequences. For instance this could apply to a range of alternative start dates.
☐ Submittal of prices for options at tender.
☐ An instant form of disputes procedure to settle issues in the event of

disagreement as construction progresses so that price variations can be agreed.

☐ An incentive to contractors to accommodate variations with minimum effect on quality, time and cost.

☐ From the employer's decision to instigate a variation, to its incorporation into the works, the response should be routed through as few hands as possible and be processed in the quickest way possible.

VALUE ENGINEERING

Value engineering has been described as the elimination of unnecessary cost which provides neither use, nor life, nor quality, nor appearance, nor employer's features. The author goes a little further by regarding it as an exercise for the employer, together with manufacturers and trade contractors, to review the design decisions made by design consultants in order to obtain the best value for money. Done effectively savings can average 10 per cent on each major trade contractor package involving specialist design. In an extreme case the author witnessed 80 per cent savings on a package involving a cleaning cradle system without any deterioration in the standard of the facility.

The most significant results of such reviews are obtained when trade contractors are competing to win an order. However, it should be recognised that the exercise requires time for research, re-design and re-assembly of pricing data. The employer must participate in the review. It is only the employer who can weigh the balance of savings against not meeting the consultant's specification. He/she may also be needed to encourage designers to change their concepts since designers become wedded to ideas and resist change.

The value engineering review generally involves talking to more than one trade contractor and setting out tender pricing documents which encourage alternatives. The documents should request a clear breakdown of the pricing particularly in respect of the pricing of risks such as currency risk, fluctuations, engineering and design development costs, district surveyor requirements and testing of mock-ups. Upon assessment it may pay the employer to introduce provisional sums (which are adjusted when the cost is known) to certain items of uncertainty, thus shouldering the risk. Tooling-up in a factory (say a brake press for metal ceiling components) generally requires a run of 10,000 items before the cost of the tooling is recovered.

Precise information is only available after the trade contractors have tendered for the project. The provision of Holorib metal floor decking can take 15 per cent off the pricing of labour costs of services and suspended ceilings etc, hung from the soffit, and yet many tender documents go out to trade contractors and suppliers without describing the structural soffit to which they will fix their installations.

A successful procurement system should provide opportunity and time for this crucial activity to take place at a point when the employer can test and select the options available from trade contractors without incurring time in penalties because changes cannot be accommodated in the programme.

CONTROL OF QUALITY AND PRODUCTION DESIGN INFORMATION

The value of excellence in design is undergoing a revival. The commercial office market took its lead from the strong tenant market in the beginning of the 1980's which put a good functional and environmentally suitable building in a fringe location above a poor building in a prime location. The retail industry was first to demonstrate that good architecture can help sell products. It was not long before more companies began to recognise that the offices they occupied reflected their image. The Orbit Reports and Broadgate Studies of the American trading markets (*The Orbit Study: Information Technology and Office Design* by Frances Duffy, DEGW, April 1983) concentrated on function and flexibility. They produced a greater awareness of quality of design effecting long term flexibility catering for expansion of information technology and consequential improved investment value flowing from good design. In the 1960s, design-build resulted in buildings which were suitable in function at that time, but lacked flexibility to cope with advancing office technology and many were aesthetic disasters.

Any procurement system which aims to involve the contractor in design has to guarantee the quality of the building and preserve continuity of the concept right through to final detailing. Cost-in-use, annual maintenance charges and future flexibility have all become important in preserving investment value in the long term. Ways of emphasising these aspects of quality need to be incorporated in procurement systems.

If a design team is under pressure because information is late, quality of design can be seriously jeopardised. There is little argument that if the cut-off point of information is embodied in the tender documentation and all further information is then the responsibility of the contractor then a major bone of contention is removed. The residual design can be executed and resourced in such a way as to allow sufficient time to incorporate quality. Additionally the main contractor is more able to take full control of the construction phase of the project if it has charge of the flow and adequacy of design information.

INCENTIVES

If the risk line is to be moved away from the general contracting industry but kept in place on trade contracts it is important that adequate incentives are provided for the main contractor to control risk under its management.

Historically, the re-introduction of risk to management contracts particularly in the field of liquidated and ascertained damages has served only to re-introduce adversarial attitudes putting the management contractor squarely on the side of trade contractors pursuing claims for extensions of time.

The estimate of prime cost (EPC) used on management contracts has been criticised. There is a suspicion that the estimated prime cost has often been set at a level of comfort where the employer's professional quantity surveyor, the architect and the contractor have adequately covered themselves and are fairly certain that the out-turn costs can be achieved. It should be noted that the EPC is agreed in advance of the 'notice to proceed' being given and often before detailed design is complete. Inherently, the EPC will contain certain contingencies for elements of the design yet to be

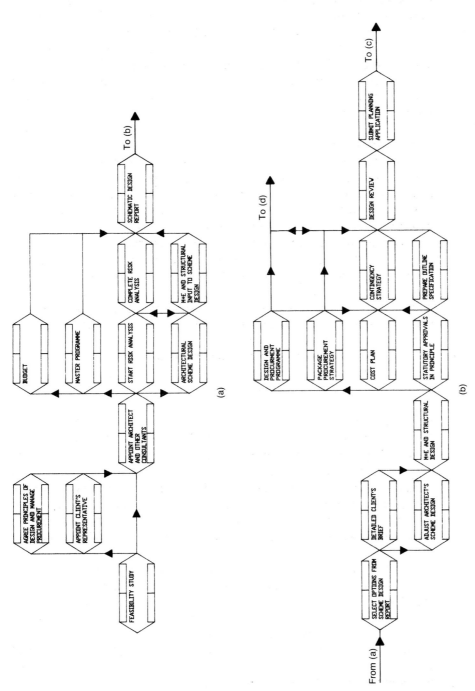

Figure 4: (a) Stage 1 – feasibility and setting up of the system; (b) stage 2 – planning; general arrangement and configuration

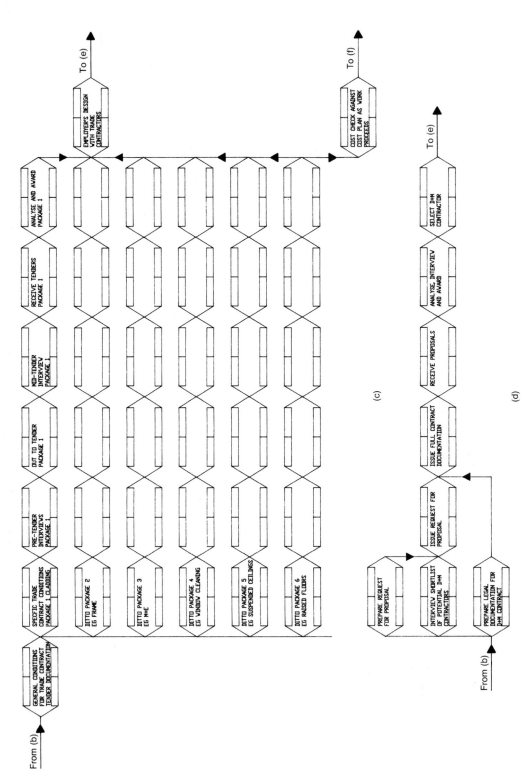

Figure 4: (c) stage 3 – detailed design with specialist trade input; (d) stage 4 – appointment of the contractor

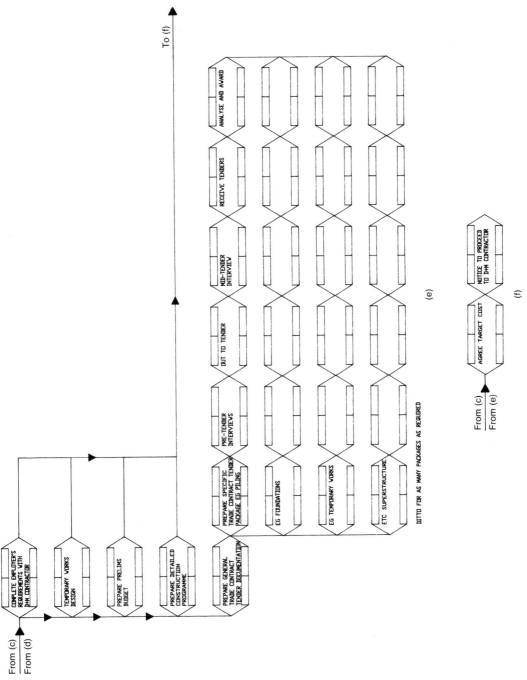

Figure 4: (e) stage 5 – preparation of the employer's requirements; (f) stage 6 – agreement of the target cost and notice to proceed

produced as well as for work designed but not yet priced. The EPC in these circumstances hardly represents an aggressive target nor is there any significant incentive for the contractor to improve on the figures agreed.

Further concerns exist over the efficient and economical use of site establishment costs generally packaged under 'preliminaries'. The overtime costs of 'general purpose' gangs and the cost of site accommodation and staff on management contracts outstrip the costs of preliminaries on traditionally competitively tendered contracts. Staff costs, for instance, on standard forms of lump-sum fixed-price contract are often estimated at 2.5 per cent of the tender price yet on management contracts staff costs are often closer to four per cent of the total EPC.

Most consultants will agree that management contracting as a system produces substantially more paper and bureaucracy than other forms of procurement. Most of the paper is to ensure that no residue of risk rests with the management contractor who often does not check the paper work but merely acts as a post box between designers and trade contractors. Much of the paper is also produced in order to satisfy the employer and its professional quantity surveyor that actual costs are authentic. The author has seen a 150 page tender document go out for the procurement of a flag pole! Accountability procedures have a history of encouraging bureaucracy as most civil servants will testify.

"The eye of the master is greatly sharpened by self interest", was an observation following the 1880 failure of management contracting to construct the Birmingham and Gloucester railway to budget or programme. It is equally true today. A successful procurement system that is cost-based should include real incentives or penalties to match efficient or inefficient performance of the contractor managing the project.

Under fixed-price procurement any savings made by a main contractor or its trade-contractor normally benefit the contractor not the employer. Under cost-based contracts there is no incentive for the contractor to make savings for the employer. It is only under target cost contracts that opportunities exist for the introduction of incentive systems for main contractors and trade contractors which provide savings for main contractors, trade contractors and employers.

THE TARGET COST DESIGN AND MANAGEMENT
PROCUREMENT SYSTEM
The system of procurement described in the next section of the book sets out to provide answers to the criteria described above. The system is broken down into eight stages, each introduced by a summary in italics for those readers who want to understand the system without examining the detail. Figure 4 illustrates the first six stages of the system. The contractor who secures the contract is called the design and management contractor, or d&m contractor, as it manages both the finalisation of the design by the design consultants and the work of the trade contractors.

Detailed procedures for a target cost d&m contract

FEASIBILITY AND SETTING UP THE SYSTEM

During Stage 1 the employer examines the feasibility of the project, explores development, planning and building options and decides whether to proceed or not. If the employer decides to proceed, an outline brief will be prepared for discussion with design and cost consultants prior to their selection; a decision is taken on the suitability of the project for the target cost design and management (d&m) contractor procurement system; a risk analysis should be carried out and a master programme prepared. Stage 1 ends with the design consultants preparing and submitting a design report to the employer which looks at the options for design and costs.

OUTLINE BRIEF

The employer examines alternatives and the viability of Planning Approval and construction. Out of this process, if the project is to proceed, will emerge a basic scheme, a budget and a schedule upon which cost appraisals have been based. This is consolidated into a document called the outline brief.

CONTRACTS

It is at this stage that alternative systems of procuring the design and construction of the project should be explored. If the employer decides to use the target cost design and management system then it needs to discuss the implications with the design team. Designers may be particularly concerned about their employment switching from the employer to the d&m contractor during the course of the contract. Generally design consultants much prefer to work for developers and do not relish working for contractors. However attitudes are changing particularly as many contractors have become developers in their own right and have a greater understanding of the motivation and management of design teams. Most large design practices have now had experience of providing services to design-build projects and many grudgingly admit that the experience was not as bad as they had initially imagined. The design professional's prejudices are often based on the experience of adversarial conflicts from working with lump-sum standard forms of contract. Under this target cost procurement system the d&m contractor requires the goodwill and co-operation of the design consultants who are able to influence the design right through to completion. Furthermore the d&m contractor must execute a contract by deed with the employer and give warranties to certain third parties. This can mean that the contractor accepts responsibility for the quality of workmanship for at least 12 years. The d&m contractor is the first party to be approached if defects occur and with increasing litigation taking place in respect of latent defects, the seriousness of such acceptance should not be underestimated.

As part of the briefing procedure the employer should provide the design consultants with drafts of the agreements and contracts. These will consist of:

- ☐ The agreement between employer and design consultants.
- ☐ The conditions of engagement between the d&m contractor and the sub-consultants (sub-consultancy agreement).
- ☐ The agreement between employer and the d&m contractor.
- ☐ The pro forma trade contract, along with all copies of proposed direct warranties to third parties.

A model architect's agreement and explanatory memoranda of the building agreements can be found in Appendices 1-3 of this manual. It is important that any conditions of engagement with design consultants tie in with the procurement method and particularly the duties to be performed by the sub-consultants under the building agreement.

Appendix 4 provides a visual guide to the duties and responsibilities of design consultants under the agreements advocated.

EMPLOYER'S MANAGEMENT

The employer must also decide how the project is to be managed. Either a member of the employer's staff may be appointed or an independent consultant. The staff member would need to have sufficient experience and be available full time on a large project. It is a demanding role from Stage 3 onwards.

The appointment of an outside consultant releases employer's staff to perform their normal duties and may provide a greater depth of technical experience. An outsider is free from internal organisational pressures and politics. On the other hand self- interest and direct employer clout are powerful weapons; a combination of the two can prove effective.

In this document the phrase 'employer's representative' has been used to denote the person who is responsible for managing the project on behalf of the employer. Where the word employer is used it either means the company responsible for commissioning the development or a director of the company.

ARCHITECT

The outline brief, if written correctly, is an ideal document for stimulating a design response from different architectural practices. As well as setting out the employer's objectives the outline brief should describe the background and history of the project particularly in respect of planning matters and legal negotiations. *The BPF Manual Appendix 2 Checklist* gives a useful aide memoire to preparing an outline brief. The ability to respond to this brief, individuality, flair and style are subjective qualities vital to achieving the desired end product. Choosing the right architect to suit a given situation requires considerable skill and judgement. A limited competition properly organised and assessed by a panel of judges can produce a good solution to development.

When choosing an architectural practice a careful assessment of the workload and available resources is vitally important. Although a team of four to six architects can take a large scheme to planning stage, once planning permission is given the initial team needs to expand rapidly. Each package will require the attention of an individual or its own small team. The skills required by these teams need to be more 'engineering and technically' orientated and less 'design' orientated than the first.

The size of the architectural team may be calculated using the data collected on the three BPF projects carried out by the author's firm Trench Farrow when one person hour of architect's time was required to develop fully the employer's requirements for every £600 (1989) value of building work. On all these projects the employer required that the design should be very well developed before it was handed to the contractor for completion. The rapid advance of CAD systems may well change this figure. Assuming the architect has the resources to meet the requirements of the project, paramount in the selection process is the quality of rapport between employer and architect. This will manifest itself during discussions when the architects display their portfolio and describe their approach to the project.

PROFESSIONAL QUANTITY SURVEYOR

The choice of professional quantity surveyor, pqs, is also important. Track record on similar projects is essential. The choice of pqs to be assigned full time to the project is as important as the partner who takes overall responsibility. Good accurate conceptual cost estimating is a rare gift and pro-active participation in design is preferable to 'passive number crunching'. Getting on with the design team but at the same time having the ability to question unnecessary expense with an occasional challenge to the designer's ego, requires personality and tact which is not in every person's make-up. Negotiating skills are also required using this procurement system.

The value and content of the building services as a proportion of whole development cost is continually increasing. Huge savings can be made however and any quantity surveying practice qualifying for appointment on a major commercial office building must employ specialists who understand both engineering and costs of mechanical and electrical services. The tendency to leave costing to the mechanical and electrical (m&e) consultant is a questionable practice and can mean that the costs of chosen solutions are never challenged. To leave budgeting and cost control to a mechanical and electrical (m&e) designer/contractor is even more questionable. The pqs is not transferred to the contractor and throughout remains guardian of the employer's purse.

STRUCTURAL AND SERVICES CONSULTANTS

There is much to be said for the architect selecting fellow design consultants; arranged marriages are risky and compatibility in a design team is essential for co-ordination. Proximity of offices and integration of computer systems also make for better communication.

CONSULTANTS' FEES

The procurement system and the proposed conditions of engagement should be made available to the consultants at the outset of fee negotiation.

Table 2: Recommended breakdown of consultancy fees when part services are carried out under d&m contractor

TERMS OF ENGAGEMENT Z%	% of FEE	BASIS OF PAYMENT
Employer's requirements under employer and paid direct by employer	50% of Z% (Half of anticipated fee)	Lump-sum against cost plan established end of Stage 2 paid quarterly during Stage(s) 3 (and 5)
Completion of design and construction under d&m contractor	40% of Z% of prime cost less retention	Payable with interim certificate (Retained value % due on making good of defects)
Employer supervision under client representative paid by the employer	10% of Z% of initial target cost agreed by d&m contractor	Lump-sum payable quarterly until certificate of making good of defects

It should be remembered that all consultants will be providing a full design service albeit partly as sub-consultants to the d&m contractor. The question of how the building works should be overseen and inspected is discussed in Stage 7 but should be decided upon at this stage.

It is recommended that 50 per cent of the consultant's fee is allocated to pay for design prior to the appointment of the d&m contractor, 40 per cent to the design controlled by the d&m contractor and the remaining 10 per cent for site inspection services. Ten per cent is adequate as site inspection duties are generally less onerous than the full contract administration role required under a *JCT 80* traditional contract. Under this system the employer's representative administers the contract.

It is recommended that some elements of this fee should be paid on a lump sum basis so that additional fees are not automatically applied on a percentage basis to d&m contractor's claims or expenditure over the pre-set budgets. Table 2 sets out the principles.

BUDGET

The budget at this stage is developed on the basis of a historical analysis of comparable buildings using final account not tender figures. Here is where a quantity surveying firm with a broad portfolio of similar and current buildings is particularly useful. The budget with its stated base date also has to match the appraisal figures produced by the employer. At this stage the elements and format in the *Building Cost Information Service (Quarterly Review of Building Prices* published by Royal Institute of Chartered Surveyors) may be used. Contingencies at this early stage ought to be 10 per cent on new build work and more on refurbishment. A clear statement of costs excluded from the building budget but which nevertheless are development costs such as local authority and design fees (or equipment provided by the client) should accompany the budget so there are no ambiguities later when a cost plan is developed. The employer can make sure that these excluded costs are incorporated somewhere in its spreadsheet of development costs. The employer will also have a shrewd idea of what competitors are paying for buildings of various standards of

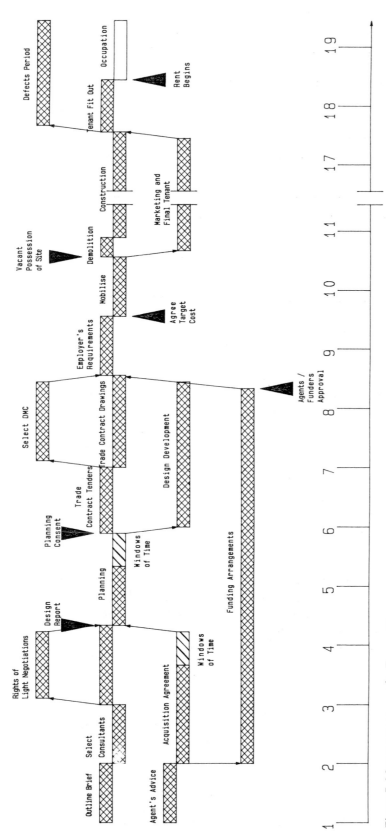

Figure 5: Master programme for Tarrow House

quality elsewhere in the region. With input also from the architect the budget is massaged and finally approved by the employer.

MASTER PROGRAMME

The master programme, Figure 5, should be drawn up by the employer and match time periods used for interest calculations which form such an important part of the development cost appraisal. It comprises a schedule of the main activities and the eight stages defined in this system of procurement. Some indefinite timescales of activities outside the control of the employer, such as negotiating time or planning approval, should be given a 'window of time', instead of a fixed point, so that best and worst timescales can be analysed particularly in respect of cash flow and interest projections.

This document is the forerunner of a far more detailed design and procurement programme and the construction programme drawn up in later stages when more information is available. It is important that times allocated in the schedule are adequate to carry out the work. A search for historical similarities in terms of programming is as important as applying comparisons to budgets. Over-ambitious time schedules can ultimately have a very harmful effect on the project and its out-turn costs. The amount of time taken to divert statutory services, close roads and construct basements should not be underestimated.

RISK ANALYSIS CHART

The employer should prepare a risk analysis chart which lists all the major risks which could occur during the course of the development. The probability of an event occurring should be listed on a scale of one to ten. The point at which each risk disappears should be noted together with the steps taken to control or transfer it. Finally, a calculation of the effects of delay and an assessment of likely costs should be made. If all events leading to loss of time or money occurred during the development it would be catastrophic. This is, of course, extremely unlikely – the laws of chance and the measures taken to mitigate the risk see to that.

Table 3 is part of a chart drawn up for a project to enable the employer to make a reasonable assessment of exposure to risk and also to allow sensible precautions to be taken to reduce the chance of the identified event taking place. For instance, the risk of abnormal ground conditions was mitigated by arranging for extensive pile tests to be carried out.

On a recent project the risk caused by placing a large cladding contract with a small German supplier was mitigated by hiring a UK warehouse to encourage and store early deliveries. The special dies used in manufacturing were purchased in advance by the employer so that in the event of the German supplier's bankruptcy, the employer could easily arrange for another manufacturer to supply the cladding.

DESIGN REPORT

Stage 1 is rounded off by the design team submitting a design report to the employer which consists of architectural schematic layouts with a number of design options supported by information on the implications for costs, schedules of space, planning restraints, occupancy and other relevant

Table 3: Typical risk analysis chart

ITEM OF RISK	COMMENTARY OF LIKELIHOOD & DISCRETE CIRCUMSTANCES TO THE PROJECT *Scale of risk 1-10*	STEPS TAKEN TO CONTROL RISK	GUESSTIMATE OF MAXIMUM COST	GUESSTIMATE OF MAXIMUM PROGRAMME DELAY	SUGGESTED CONTINGENCY
1 Noise and nuisance actions	Biggs & Co. have shown every indication that they intend to pursue legal actions against the contractor and employer *Scale 9*	1. Compensation offered & refused. 2. Environmental Health Officer brought in – Section 60 notice served restraining certain noisy operations to time periods and noise limit	1. If 9 hr day reduced to 6 hrs on noisy operations **£550,000** 2. If 50% time added to all noisy operations **£1.35m** 3. If catastrophic & reduced to 24 hr night working on £15m of work inc superstructure **£3.40m** 4. If piling foundations goes to 12 hr night shifts (£2000 per rig per night) **£600,000**	6 Weeks 15 Weeks 41 Weeks 4 Weeks	£300,000
2 Abnormal ground conditions causing collapse of reamed pile excavations	In the borehole tests we suffered a collapsed borehole. However, it is not known whether the collapse occurred within 1 hr or 10 hrs of excavation by the augur rig. Engineer's instinct was to specify the much more expensive "friction pile solution throughout" at a huge cost in programme & money. The design calls for 100 piles with 58 underreamed *Scale 6*	Price & programme obtained for options under competitive tender.	1. Failure on Day 1 **£3.60m** 2. Change after 50% of underreams **£2.8m**	28 Weeks 22 Weeks	£750,000
3 Unforeseen ground obstructions from old foundations/bases & the like	Prototype pile showed up an unexpected obstruction below formation level *Scale 6*	Probing at setting out position of each pile before rigs commence work	Worst scenario **£420,000** (Note: Archeology risk elsewhere)	4 Weeks	£200,000
4 Standing & tidal water	River now underground receives water from as far away as Hampstead – the Office Court West drainage chamber 6 years ago rose to a level of 18 ft *Scale 3*	De-watering pumps could be brought in	**£100,000**	1 Week	
5 Exceptionally adverse weather conditions	1988 winter one of the warmest & dryest on record. Should be out of the ground by summer *Scale 4*		**£60,000**	1 Week	

continued on next page

Table 3 – continued from previous page

ITEM OF RISK	COMMENTARY OF LIKELIHOOD & DISCRETE CIRCUMSTANCES TO THE PROJECT *Scale of risk 1-10*	STEPS TAKEN TO CONTROL RISK	GUESSTIMATE OF MAXIMUM COST	GUESSTIMATE OF MAXIMUM PROGRAMME DELAY	SUGGESTED CONTINGENCY
6 Archeological finds	The majority of the site is not being excavated below previously excavated level. Museum of London have not expressed an interest. Therefore unlikely *Scale 2*	Previous owner did not consider this to be a risk	De minimus		
7 Adjacent property heave or subsidence	Temporary works design by the contractor. Permanent works designed by consultant. Both are liable if negligence is proven *Scale 1*	Covered by employer insurance	De minimus		
8 Injury to persons or property	Contractor covers his own liability. A probability but of a minor nature *Scale 1*	Covered by employer insurance	De minimus		
9 Fire or collapse of structures	*Scale 1*	Covered by employer insurance	De minimus		
10 Retained facade of building	Very little is retained – new structural floor restraints it before old lateral restraints are cut away *Scale 1*	Covered by insurance	De minimus		
11 Bankruptcy of Management Contractor	Unlikely – the asset base of contractor parent co. includes a substantial property base *Scale 1*	Parent company guarantee has been given to employer	De minimus		
12 Tower crane air rights compensation	A recent "sticks in my gullet" judgement in Docklands has alerted people to their rights & escalated compensation payments *Scale 2*	Minimum radii of tower cranes. Luffing jib cranes uneconomical even against compensation payments	20 properties at £10,000 each £200,000	De minimus	
13 Civil commotion, war, nuclear peril & force majeure	Act of God *Scale 1*	Cannot insure	De minimus	De minimus	
14 Adjacent owners – compensation for nuisance – redecoration & cleaning expenses	Biggs & Co. have asked for cleaning. Lawyers in Office Court West are actively pursuing claims. Individuals have been put up in hotels *Scale 1*	Good neighbour policy of informing them what is going on by Contractor. Negotiate best deal where possible	£250,000	De minimus	

Item	Comment	Action	Detail / Value	Weeks	Cost
15 Change in tender information by Statutory Authorities during design development	Has happened on practically every job in London to a smaller or greater degree. Some interpretation of bylaws is subjective and left to local officers. *Scale 9*	Employment of top consultants who know the system. As much consultation as possible prior to tendering	£600,000	8 Weeks	£300,000
16 Timing of final design consultants' information	If works contractors lose money this is the easiest avenue to pursue. If programme is affected the management contractor will support the works contractors to avoid penalties *Scale 9*	Detailed tracking of design team performance by employer and employer's representative	£3.6m	20 Weeks	£500,000
17 Access to front buildings & benefit of some shared resources in preliminary overheads	This is a matter of timing. There is a window of time in respect of economical access & the construction of Tarrow S.E. structure *Scale 3*	Separately resourced. Design team being assembled to undertake design work. Once assembled a schedule of dates will be prepared	Front building's effective subsidy on Tarrow House overheads (i.e 1/3 of planning engineer's time etc) £500,000	De minimus	£100,000
18 Bankruptcy or liquidation of works contractors or major supplier	The market currently is overheated. However this means profit margins have risen. Labour rates in London are rising in some cases as much as 20% in a year. Works contracts are being let 'fixed price'. In the case of the German cladding contractor we have placed an order of £16m. His last year turnover was £40m *Scale 3*	Performance bonds are being requested as well as parent co. guarantees on all large orders placed. d&m contractor staff are being pressed to reside in Germany for the course of the contract	If trade contractor went into liquidation half way through manufacture £6.5m	50 weeks	
19 Adequacy of design consultant's information & changes made during design development & production drawings prepared by trade contractors. Problem areas: Tolerance & interface between packages	The early packages developed without the benefit of construction information developed later are most at risk: i.e. steel was tendered before GS value engineering exercise was completed & prior to resolution of cladding details *Scale 8*	Continual pressure on designers for complete information from: 1 Client 2 Employer's representative 3 Main contractor	Steel 15% £780,000 Cladding 5% £800,000 M&e services 7.5% £975,000 Courtyard glazing 5% £60,000 SS Windows/doors £75,000 Remainder 3% £1.7m £4,390,000	40 weeks	£2,000,000

continued on next page

Table 3 – continued from previous page

ITEM OF RISK	COMMENTARY OF LIKELIHOOD & DISCRETE CIRCUMSTANCES TO THE PROJECT *Scale of risk 1-10*	STEPS TAKEN TO CONTROL RISK	GUESSTIMATE OF MAXIMUM COST	GUESSTIMATE OF MAXIMUM PROGRAMME DELAY	SUGGESTED CONTINGENCY
20 Quantity risk	Package information & Bills of Quantities are being prepared by PQS. Tenderers could claim if quantities are exceeded *Scale 8*	d&m contractor checks PQS documentation	Concrete, Brickwork, Plaster, Floor screed, Dry lining, Handset stone } £500,000	De minimis	£100,000
21 Underpinning existing buildings – unforeseen conditions	Only a small area of underpinning under shop area *Scale 3*		£50,000	1/2 week	
22 Tendering climate	£30m left to tender. Market is very overheated in the UK. Inflation allowance may not be enough on certain packages & difficulties in obtaining good competitive bids may occur *Scale 3*	Looking at Europe & USA for competition. Extensive pre-tender interviews to establish keenness of bidders taking place	£30m + extra 4% £1.2m	No effect	
23 Trade contractor performance risk	Delay by one works contractor and its 'knock on' disruption, prolongation & programme costs to other contractors & the project: a) Labour resources are in dangerously short supply b) Local/national or dock strikes can happen c) The imposition of suppliers by the client/design team on to works contractor does not make for unison & loyalty if materials are in short supply *Scale 9*	Picking trade contractors with good record. Planning & site management under d&m contractor being pressurised to perform. Liquidated & ascertained damages (penalty clauses) are part of works contract conditions; however these run at a max. of £50,000 per week & in many cases are reduced in order to obtain a bid	In the last overheated period of the 1960's contracts generally met delays that added 10% to the contract sum £7m	52 weeks	£4,000,000
24 Defective work or design	This usually shows up in the early stages (first five years) of occupation *Scale 7*	All consultants' agreements are signed under seal (12 years liability) & 'care & diligence' clauses would mean suing for negligence. (Professional indemnity insurance checked) d&m contractor has similar obligations. Trade contractors with 'design' input give direct warranties	A year's defects liability period covers 'workmanship' and materials £5m		£200,000
25 Flood	Buildings can flood from accidents during installation of services. In a shell & core scenario the damage is less than when fitted out. Accidental floods most often occur during testing & commissioning periods *Scale 4*	24 hour security should minimise damage. Covered by insurance	Losses not covered by insurance £750,000	De minimis	£25,000
				TOTAL	£8,475,000

factors. The report should outline any additional research to be done and recommend appointment of any specialist consultants. Statements confirming the budget and programme should be included in the report. The report should recommend no more than six suitable candidates for the role of d&m contractor.

PLANNING CONSENT – GENERAL ARRANGEMENT AND CONFIGURATION

The employer reviews the options described in the design report, selects those that meet its requirements and produces a detailed brief setting out a schedule of requirements and standards. The consultants develop scheme drawings accommodating both structural and building services. Cores and space for services and circulation are also developed to the extent that net to gross calculations have some validity. Building regulations and statutory requirements are considered, particularly in respect of means of escape. Basement and roof drawings are developed to the extent that all mechanical and electrical plant, including lift equipment can be accommodated. The employer approves the scheme which is submitted for Town and Country Planning Consent.

During this stage the pqs and design consultants outline the initial packaging strategy for obtaining trade contract tenders and the preliminary budget is turned into a cost plan which matches the packaging strategy. A procurement programme for the preconstruction stage tying in to a notional construction programme is also formulated. Finally the proposed outline specification is produced for approval by the employer. This outline specification is the forerunner of a document suitable for marketing to tenants for lease agreements and for future purchasers or funding institutions.

PLANNING CONSENT

The procedures for obtaining a planning consent and the parameters of 'permitted development' are explained clearly in the manual entitled *Planning Applications: The RMJM Guide* (published by BSP Professional Books). The degree of detail required by planning officers and their committees varies between authorities, largely depending on:

☐ The size of the proposed scheme.
☐ The complexity and location of the scheme.
☐ The political and social impact and sensitivity of the scheme and its relationship to regional and local structure plans.
☐ The prejudices of the allocated planning officer and the constituents of the committee.

Before preparing planning applications the architect and the employer are advised to discuss the proposed submission with the planning officer and seek out the planning committee's likely attitude to different approaches. As a scheme begins to formulate it is important to have early discussion with the borough engineer to establish requirements for site access, traffic, parking and building control.

THIRD PARTY NEGOTIATION

It is as well to begin negotiations at an early stage. In this way, a more favourable settlement is likely to accrue because once planning drawings are submitted they can be publicly scrutinised and commented upon. Part of the strength of the employer's hand in negotiations is the ability, if necessary, to design a building that avoids or mitigates the severity or impact of specific problems, e.g. claims in respect of rights of light or the purchase of surrounding property.

EMPLOYER SANCTION OF PLANNING SUBMISSION

The planning drawings should be carefully checked by the employer to see that its requirements have been met for net usable areas of good flexible space, accommodation of plant, standards of natural light and finish and reasonable maintenance and operational costs. The employer will also need a statement confirming that the planning drawings will produce a building within the agreed budget.

DEVELOPMENT OF GENERAL ARRANGEMENT AND CONFIGURATION DRAWINGS

During the lull while the planning process takes its course, it is worthwhile putting the drawings developed for planning consent on to a CAD system – this may, of course, result in some revised work to take account of planning committee requirements. It is also the right time for a detailed site survey and ground investigation. The detailed site survey information can be fed into the CAD system which will give the structural and services engineer a head start. CAD, which has the advantage of being able to work at any scale in three dimensions, assists avoidance of clashes in the general arrangement of the work of different disciplines from the outset. It transposes the creative freehand flow of the architect into the more regimented point to point process of engineering and provides locational accuracy during the development of the design.

By using CAD, the design work from earlier stages is dimensionally co-ordinated. An early concentration on basement and roof level work including plant room areas will pay dividends – as will the detailed design of cores. Having settled the structure and spatial provisions for services the next priority is to draw up cladding profiles for the project and its general performance specification. Throughout this period there should be constant reference back to the detailed brief to ensure that adequate provisions are being made to meet it. Provisions such as space for future kitchen ventilation by an office block tenant on each floor can easily be forgotten in the hurly burly of design.

COST AND VALUE

While the design works proceed the pqs should be commenting on 'value for money' aspects of the emerging design: the cut and fill aspects of excavations, the cost of shape, repetition and one-offs, floor to wall ratios and cost in use. The employer or its marketing agents should be commenting on bad use of space, flexibility for different envisaged uses, intrusions which spoil space, natural light etc. Comparative studies should take place during this period to select the major engineering systems, steel versus concrete for the structure, VAV versus fan coil system for air conditioning, raft versus piling for the foundations and stick construction versus factory panel units for cladding etc.

PROCUREMENT STRATEGY AND PROGRAMME

As the detail of the building emerges the pqs and consultants should be developing a package strategy for the 80 to 100 packages that are necessary in a large commercial building. Those packages requiring early design input from specialist trade contractors providing cladding systems, lifts and building services should be identified as soon as possible. This will

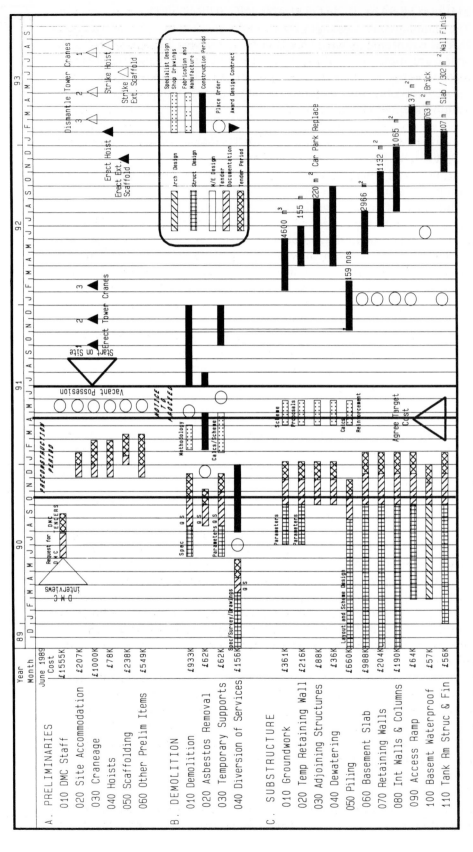

Figure 6: Example of part of a design procurement programme – Stage 2

determine the sequence in which trade contractors should come aboard in order to develop the design logically. It is not always one of the more familiar packages that is to be let first. In an extreme case the author was involved in a project where the building cleaning systems had such implications on the roof, structure and cladding design that it became the first package to be tendered. The package strategy is developed into a design procurement and construction programme. Generous periods should be allowed for trade contractor tenders and evaluation and shop drawing approval. Adequate time should be allowed for the appointment of the contractor, and off and on-site fabrication.

Part of a design procurement programme is shown in Figure 6.

COST PLAN
The packaging strategy should be developed with the cost plan. The cost plan should be reconciled with the approved budget. Figures for each package should show both the base figure (used in the budget) and the figure expected at the time of receiving each trade contractor tender. This will incorporate a figure for inflation taking account of the time for works to be manufactured and installed on site. The cost plan should show the anticipated base management fee for the d&m contractor. It should list all the background data used in its composition and exclusions considered to be outside the building budget. Rudimentary quantities should be indicated package by package with a brief description of materials. Two examples of such a cost plan are shown in Tables 4 and 5.

CONTINGENCY STRATEGY
A contingency figure ranging from ten per cent to three per cent should be allocated for each package. This involves judgement on how far the design has been developed at the time of producing the cost plan, and its likely complexity.

The figure will depend on how much change is likely to occur as a result of further information emerging after the package is let. For instance steelwork invariably goes up in weight as further aspects of the design, particularly cladding, emerge. More holes are required by the building services consultant and end connections become more complex – it probably requires a ten per cent contingency. The cost of decoration on the other hand can be forecast more accurately and a two per cent contingency may be felt to be adequate. In addition, a two per cent overall contingency should be allowed to deal with inter-package problems on site and for overtime payments to speed up the works if necessary to mitigate losses in programme.

At this stage there should be a ten per cent contingency overall - three per cent for changes prior to publication of the employer's requirements and seven per cent for the d&m contractor during the construction stage. In the case of an extensive refurbishment where the integrity of the structure, cladding and retention of services are an issue, the contingency should be even higher than ten per cent.

SCHEME DESIGN REPORT
Following receipt of planning consent, work in Stage 2 should be rounded off by the design team consolidating all their work into a scheme design

Table 4: Foundations detail of cost plan

TARROW HOUSE: FOUNDATIONS	QUANTITY	UNIT COST £	TOTAL £
West of Sewer: Piling			
Allow for:			
A Bringing plant to site; maintaining; clearing away on completion	Item		15,000
B Testing piles	Item		0
Bored cast in piles			
C 750mm diameter; 16.50m long	8 No.	1,270	10,160
D 750mm diameter; 25.00m long	6 No.	1,890	11,340
E 1000mm diameter; 1650m long	1 No.	2,550	2,550
F 1000mm diameter; 25.00m long	3 No.	3,825	11,475
G 1000mm diameter; 27.00m long	27 No.	4,050	109,350
H 1200mm diameter; 27.00m long	7 No.	4,350	30,450
I 1500mm diameter; 37.00m long	2 No.	10,000	20,000
J Reinforcement	111.36 t	650	72,384
K Cutting off heads of piles and preparing reinforcement	54 No.	60	3,240
L Clear away spoil arising from piling works	1114m³	17	18,938
Preparing heads of existing under-reamed piles			
M 1250mm diameter	14 No.	100	1,400
N 1500mm diameter	17 No.	100	1,700
O 2000mm diameter	2 No.	100	200
Sub total			308,187
Contingency @ 6%			18,491
TOTAL			326,678

Table 5: Cladding detail of cost plan

		QUANTITY	UNIT COST £	TOTAL £
TARROW HOUSE: EXTERNAL CLADDING				
To Cores 1 and 5: Precast lightweight concrete rates				
Backing panels to stone cladding; casting in stainless steel channels (provided by bracketing manufacturer); normal size 3.048m wide; insitu concrete stitching between panels				
A	300mm thick	3250 m²	330	1,072,500
B	Extra; preformed trapezoidal duct panel extreme size 3200 x 1200mm	115 m	500	57,500
C	300mm thick; to fire fighting lifts (option 1)	1016 m²	330	335,280
Cladding to Cores 1 and 5: European or American limestone; 8mm joints				
D	75mm thick; bracketing measured separately	3250 m²	275	893,750
E	Extra; edge condition at roofs; horizontal	27 m	40	1,080
F	Extra; edge condition at roofs; sloping	41 m	40	1,640
G	Extra; edge condition at acute angle; vertical; including additional brackets and labour	120 m	40	4,800
H	Extra; pointing and waterproofing around vertical louvres	422 m	25	10,550
I	75mm thick; to fire fighting lift walls; bracketing measured separately	1016 m²	275	279,400
J	Extra; edge condition at roof; horizontal	22 m	40	880
K	Extra; edge condition at right angle; vertical; including all additional brackets and labour	243 m	40	9,720
Stainless steel: support and restraint brackets				
L	To support stone cladding; to Cores 1 and 5 walls (50mm cavity)	3250 m²	40	130,000
Sub total				2,797,100
Contingency @ 7%				195,797
TOTAL				2,992,897

report. This consists of all the drawings and outline specifications from the three principal consultants, architect, building services engineer and structural engineer. The scheme design report which includes an outline specification of work is the forerunner of:

- ☐ The employer's requirements – documentation which describes the scope of the contract and the basis of the target cost.
- ☐ The tenants or users specification used in marketing and in lease negotiations and rent reviews.
- ☐ The description of the building for use in any purchase or funding agreements.

The outline specification is therefore the start of a technical specification describing all elements of the building and performance criteria. The detailed cost report is a sensitive document and should be kept separate from the scheme design report which will be circulated widely to third parties including potential contractors.

It is often worthwhile spending some money publishing and printing the scheme design report in a clear and concise fashion and binding it in a hard cover. It then becomes a document which can be used to sell the scheme not only to contractors and trade contractors but also to tenants or potential funding organisations. The process of bringing specification drawings and design rationale into one well presented document gives a substantial boost to the morale of the design team. It also draws out and helps to develop the co-ordination qualities of the design team as it works to meet the publication deadline. On a large project printing and publication costs can be in the order of £10,000 to £15,000 (1989).

DETAILED DESIGN WITH SPECIALIST TRADE INPUT

The objective of this stage is to complete the employer's end of the design process using the input from specialist trade contractors at the most appropriate time to prevent duplication or abortive design effort. By the early marriage of manufacturers, suppliers and designers it is possible to produce certainty in the onward detailing of the scheme. Crucial packages of work are interfaced with each other at a much earlier stage than is traditional and the true costs of the scheme are known before work commences on site. This gives the contractor in due course a strong base on which to agree a target cost. Additionally it gives the opportunity for the employer to study how trade contractors price the consultant's design and to review value and cost within the elemental breakdown of each major trade package. All this is expressed in detail by the party which will manufacture and install the works in due course.

TRADE CONTRACTOR PRE-TENDER INTERVIEWS

The suitability of trade contractors is established by obtaining information on their:

- ☐ Track record on similar work with references.
- ☐ Financial standing (ideally no one contract should represent more than 20 per cent of the trade contractor's annual turnover).
- ☐ Available resources and workload with particular reference to design resources.
- ☐ General approach to the scheme and how much they themselves subcontract.
- ☐ Usual suppliers.

At an initial interview the broad outline of the scheme, the scope of the package and the system being used for procurement is explained. The trade contractor takes away the scheme design report and an explanatory memorandum of the pro forma trade contract and is asked to confirm his/her interest in tendering.

TRADE CONTRACTOR TENDER DOCUMENTATION

To get specialist and trade contractors to contribute effectively to the design, specifications should be performance based and drawings should be detailed in such a way as to encourage options and innovation. Obviously the profiles and visual finish of a cladding system should be defined by the architect but how it is achieved or fixed should be left to the trade contractor. If a d&m contractor has not been appointed at this stage the professional quantity surveyor (pqs) in conjunction with the employer's representative and legal adviser provides all the conditions of sub-contract normally provided by a main contractor in a fixed-price contract. This includes a list of key dates and a schedule for accomplishing design fabrications and site fixing together with a list of attendance and services to be provided by the contractor.

Trade contractor tender documents should consist of eleven items:

- ☐ The form of tender.
- ☐ A mandatory pricing schedule which should include a day work provision set at say ten per cent of site fixing labour costs.
- ☐ Hourly rates for designers and draughtsmen.

☐ Instructions to tenderers and general information and conditions including (if appropriate):
  - Instructions.
  - Key dates of programme.
  - Sequence of working.
  - The names of other trade contractors working in parallel.
  - Drawing submissions.
  - Prices.
  - Schedule of drawings.
  - The names of contractors under consideration.
  - Trade contract programme.
  - Information provided by others.
  - Ordering of materials.
  - Work outside site boundary.
  - Payments.
  - Covering varied works.
  - Trade contractors' huts, plant and materials.
☐ Trade contractors' obligations including:
  - Working hours.
  - Labour.
  - Industrial relations.
  - Safety.
  - Site security.
  - Protection of public and private services.
  - Adjacent occupiers and property.
  - Cleaning and site clearance.
  - Unloading and handling.
  - Effluents and waste.
  - Reporting to the d&m contractor.
  - Accident procedures.
  - Previous work by others.
  - Progress photographs and cinema-tographic film records.
  - Statutory and regulating authorities.
  - Protection.
  - Setting out.
  - Temporary weather conditions.
  - Winter building.
  - Maintenance of public roads and footpaths.
  - Site access roads.
  - Scaffolding.
  - Daywork.
  - Failure to comply.
  - Damage to work of others.
  - Subletting work.
  - Fire precautions.
☐ Attendance and service to be provided by the d&m contractor including:
  - Scope.
  - Welfare.
  - Temporary telephones.
  - Temporary electric lighting and electricity.

- Temporary water supply.
- Vehicle access and parking.
- Removal of rubbish.
- Temporary signboard and advertising.
- Common user services and schedule.

☐ General specification and requirements (to be provided by architect for each trade package). Engineering performance specification (to be provided by the consulting engineer for each appropriate trade package).

☐ Schedule of tender drawings (list to be compiled by architect and design consultants for each trade package).

☐ Other information to be completed by the tenderer (to be looked at in each case by the employer's representative and design team).

☐ Explanatory memorandum of the pro forma trade contract.

☐ Explanatory memorandum of the contractor's agreement (the *D&M Contractor's Agreement*). Because of the length and legal language of the full text of the bespoke contracts, a readable and user friendly document capable of being read and understood by estimators and managing directors without recourse to lawyers is required when pricing commences. This obviates the need for documents to be sent to lawyers for interpretation. The full text of both contracts are handed over either at mid-tender interviews or dispatched some ten working days before tenders are due to be returned so that contractors may check in detail what is paraphrased in the explanatory memorandum.

Explanatory memoranda of the *D&M Contractor's Agreement* and the *Pro forma Trade Contract* produced by Nabarro Nathanson are contained in Appendices 2 and 3 at the back of this manual.

MID-TENDER TRADE CONTRACT INTERVIEWS
It is important for appropriate members of the design team and the pqs to meet each tenderer three quarters of the way through the trade contractor tender period to answer any questions on the documentation and to comment on the tenderer's approach to the design. This helps to lower the trade contractor's perception of risk which will help to reduce prices. In these discussions the pqs must decide what should be kept confidential to one tenderer and what constitutes a concession in specification and therefore should be published as an addendum and passed to all tenderers. As soon as an addendum is published, all tenderers have a tendency to request at least two weeks' extension of the tender period. It is in the employer's interest to grant further time rather than accept provisional sums, and programmes should allow slack for this eventuality. Failure to extend the time may lead to tenderers qualifying their bids or inserting provisional sums. This is not in the employer's interest since tenderers often exchange information on their bids following submittal. Trying to negotiate withdrawal of qualifications when each tenderer knows its competitor's price is undesirable.

TRADE CONTRACTOR TENDER EVALUATION AND SELECTION
The tenders submitted by the trade contractors should be copied and issued by the pqs to the employer's representative and the appropriate design

consultants as quickly as possible. The design team needs to examine the technical substance of all drawings, manuals or descriptive literature and specifications of all tenderers. Meanwhile the pqs examines the figures, qualification and options that have been submitted, arranging them on a like-for-like basis with as much detail as possible. Having received technical appraisals from the design team, the pqs produces a tender report recommending two trade contractors for ongoing tender review meetings.

The employer's representative generally attends those meetings when prices are clarified (particularly those associated with risk) and the design is discussed. Risk items that attract high prices may be better dealt with as provisional sums thus making them 'cost reimbursable' items rather than 'priced risk' items. This includes the inflation element of a fixed price or, say, currency fluctuations. As much information as possible is gleaned from the tenderers in respect of the proposed design and quality of the product they are offering, the make-up of their prices and of any sub-contracted and supplier costs.

While still in competition, the two most suitable tenderers are encouraged to put forward alternatives that produce better value for money while meeting the design intent. Every avenue should be explored to avoid the manufacture of special items and to obtain maximum output of standard runs. Wastage factors and the possibility of including the features of one package with another should be analysed. Fixing and structural characteristics should be examined before placing an order as the responsibility for fixing is very often at the demarcation between two trade contractors. For example the responsibility for the fixings of cladding must be clearly defined between the steel supplier and the cladding supplier.

Because most major trade contractors have assembled their tenders from many suppliers and sub-contractors it is necessary to hold more than one meeting to arrive at a final price and to choose a trade contractor for each package. These meetings provide an opportunity to lower costs and maintain quality by seeking innovative and cost effective solutions. This process of value engineering needs time and determined questioning and probing to achieve significant results. As soon as it is apparent that a 'one horse race' exists the second contender should not have its time wasted in fruitless exercises.

Finally a document should be prepared, carefully listing the criteria and final price agreed in tender negotiations. This, with the tender submission, forms part of the trade contract documentation. The *Pro Forma Trade Contract* including the forms of warranty is then signed between employer and trade contractor. It should be noted that the employer can terminate the trade contract at any time prior to site installation paying for costs of services to that date. This effectively ensures that design development does not become an opportunity to raise prices.

BUILDING ENVIRONMENTAL SERVICES
The increasing importance of building services in terms of its cost package size relative to the total cost plan is evident in all commercial buildings. There have been rapid technical advances in electronic controls coupled with a wish to fully automate buildings as well as their energy and life safety systems. This is producing buildings of increasing complexity. Indeed there are now very few projects where the management of the

design and installation of services does not have a major impact on the overall programme and final account.

Table 6 illustrates three different routes of procuring the design and installation of environmental services. The choice of route largely depends on the judgement of teams available and whether the project requires an innovative or standard response. In assessing the skill of design practices it must be remembered that mechanical, public health, electrical and control engineering are four different specialist skills seldom held by a single individual.

The main variable is the vital question of which party is going to produce co-ordinated design/working drawings. The author has seen this issue fudged on a number of contracts often under the pretext that it saves money; for instance jobs have been completed by moving directly from scheme drawing stage to trade contractor shop drawings. The cost of this shortcut has proved very expensive. Site co-ordination has been a nightmare and the quality has suffered. The co-ordinated drawings can be prepared by consultant or contractor providing a main mechanical and electrical contractor is employed. If however the job is to be directly let in split down packages such as ductwork, sprinklers, pipework, drainage, insulation etc; then the co-ordinated drawings should be produced by the consultant either under the employer, if the time in the preconstruction stage allows, or under the d&m contractor if it is to be carried out in the construction stage. Ideally the target cost is agreed with the d&m contractor with the availability of co-ordinated design/working drawings since the design development required for these drawings often produces changes in respect of the scheme design. It is the co-ordinated design drawings which establish accurate information in respect of the majority of the 'builders' work', requirements such as holes, access provision, plinths etc. which work out at about seven per cent of the mechanical and electrical costs and require co-ordination with other packages of work.

Initially the building services consultant's drawings and specifications should be sufficiently detailed to enable the architect and structural consultant's design to progress in a co-ordinated fashion. This means the employer should initially engage and pay the services consultant on 'abridged duties' as described in the ACE Conditions of Engagement (published by the Association of Consulting Engineers, 1981) in order to prepare tender information for mechanical and electrical packages. The building services design must be sufficiently detailed so that trade contractors can price the work without using provisional sums. Thus the services will be shown on consultants' co-ordinated design drawings and include sizes, flow rates, capacities, routes and duties of plant and equipment.

If building services are to be split into packages without an overseeing m&e contractor the consultant should oversee co-ordination on behalf of the d&m contractor. Alternatively, the ductwork contractor may be paid an extra fee for co-ordinating drawings and be given the title of 'lead contractor'. As the biggest user of space, the ductwork contractor should take responsibility for seeing that light fittings, drainage and sprinklers etc. have space allocated within the service voids so that clashes are obviated. To do this properly the additional fee paid to the ductwork contractor is about 50p per square foot (1989) of net lettable building on, say, a commercial office block if fitted out for occupation. Where an overseeing

Table 6: Routes for procuring environmental services

OPTIONS UNDER EMPLOYER	VARIES (dependent on lead-in time)	OPTIONS UNDER D&M CONTRACT		OPTIONS UNDER CLIENT'S REPRESENTATION
SCHEME DESIGN TENDER DOCUMENTS	CO-ORDINATED WORKING DRAWINGS (inc builders' work drawings)	SHOP FABRICATION TRADE INSTALLATION DRAWINGS	AS BUILT DRAWINGS	WITNESSING AND CERTIFICATION
1 Services consultant (abridged duties only) works for employer includes builders' work holes in structure over 150mm	a) Single m&e or b) M&e contractors (under d&m contractor)	Individual trade contractors, fabricators and manufacturers (under principal m&e supervision)	M&e principal contractor	Services consultant under employer's representative
2 Services consultant inc. builders' work holes in structure over 150mm (full duties working for the employer and switching to d&m contractor)	Services consultant (no main services contractor) switch from employer depends on length of pre-construction period	Trade contractor drawings split into packages (Ductwork gives lead role) coordinated by d&m contractor and sub-consultant	External agency as a package under d&m contractor and sub-consultant	External commissioning and inspectorate agency directly employed by employer and under employer's representative
3 M&e design contractor inc. builders' work holes in structure over 150mm (contracted to produce design/tender within budget and cost ground rules agreed at outset)	M&e contractor (under employer if pre-construction period allows – goes under d&m contractor upon agreement of target cost)	Individual trade contractors, fabricators and manufacturers (under control of m&e contractor under d&m contractor)	M&e contractor	External commissioning and inspectorate agency directly employed by employer and under the employer's representative

building services contractor is appointed there is no sense in switching the services consultant to working for the design contractor. The building services contractor in these circumstances would be responsible for producing co-ordinated working drawings prior to trade contractors starting their shop drawings.

TRADE CONTRACT

Once each trade contract has been awarded, the employer or the employer's representative acts as the contract administrator until such time as the contract is novated to the d&m contractor. Payments are linked to pre-agreed key points in design and fabrication when these activities take place prior to the 'notice to proceed'. Pre-agreed off-site payments should be subject to certificates of indemnity and transference of ownership. There should be direct warranties (which have the facility for novation to a future tenant or occupier) put in place for all major trade contracts backed up either by a parent company guarantee or a performance bond to the value of not less than 15 per cent of the trade contract value. The cost of this bond will represent some 1.5 per cent of the tender sum.

The *Pro Forma Trade Contract* has many similarities with *JCT 80* or the works contract to a *JCT 87 Management Contract*. The trade contractor, however, will be deemed to take responsibility for any demands made by the district surveyor and building control in respect of 'component' design. Examples of this might be in the choice, at the tender pricing stage, of exit signs or fire dampers. Risk in respect of total systems and general arrangements shown on the consultants' drawings such as staircase pressurisation or means of escape remain with the employer. Changes of any of the latter items would necessitate a variation order.

Reasons for granting extensions of time to the trade contractor are in line with most forms of traditional contract such as JCT 80. However shortage of labour, materials and exceptionally inclement weather would not qualify for setting revised completion dates for the trade contract works. Trade contractors are to be paid within 21 days of the employer's certificate being received by the d&m contractor. The author's past experience suggests that this can lead to a cash flow advantage to the d&m contractor worth 0.5 per cent on prime cost throughout an eight month £20 million contract. Disputes on time or money can be referred to an appointed adjudicator during the contract and taken to the High Court, if necessary, after practical completion.

TRADE CONTRACTOR DESIGN UNDER THE DESIGN TEAM

Once appointed, each trade contractor attends design sessions with the appropriate members of the design team. Each trade contractor contributes to the development of the design relating to its area of special expertise under the sanction of the appropriate design consultant. The trade contractor's work with the design team is normally completed when its key drawings are developed (particularly fixings, junctions and abutments). At this point the pqs has enough information to confirm the details of the price of the interfaces between the trade contractors' packages.

Any variations during this period must be brought to the attention of the employer's representative. During this period mock-ups and samples may be tested, thus removing any unjustifiable risk in respect of technical inadequacy occurring during the construction period.

APPOINTMENT OF THE D&M CONTRACTOR

The timing of the appointment of a d&m contractor depends on the lead-in time for design but it is not recommended to select a d&m contractor more than say seven months before the start on site. This is because the contractor's key personnel cannot be guaranteed or spared on preconstruction activities over a longer period. Furthermore, costs of preconstruction services range from £25,000 to £40,000 (1990) a month and are hard to justify in respect of benefit over a longer period. Information on contractor's programme, site facilities and sub-contract conditions applicable to the trade contracts can be agreed, if necessary, by consensus between all contractors on the shortlist in advance of a request for a proposal. Certain trade contracts require detailed planning and method studies which each d&m contractor might approach differently. Substructure and reinforced concrete superstructure work should therefore not be tendered until the d&m contractor is appointed. Buildability and design advice on cladding, lifts and services will be given by trade contractors already signed up with the employer and working with the design team.

A request for a proposal is circulated to not more than six contractors. It seeks competitive tenders for a base fee to be applied to prime cost throughout the construction period and asks what percentage range of slide the contractors are prepared to offer under the target cost incentive mechanism. It could also request a guaranteed maximum price under competition if the scope of tender document is sufficient to define quantity and quality. The contractor is also asked to quote a lump sum for preconstruction services. The request for a proposal sets out the proposed contingencies to be applied to each package in the assembly of the target cost and seeks out any changes demanded by the contractor. It asks what quality, numbers and costs of staff are to be employed. It seeks confirmation that the contractor is prepared to adopt the trade contracts, and the d&m agreement including the terms of the proposed d&m contractor/sub-consultants agreements already negotiated and pre-agreed between employer and consultants.

The contractor is selected following assessment of the proposals and a rigorous interviewing procedure.

TIMING OF THE APPOINTMENT

The timing of the appointment of the contractor will depend upon the views of the employer's representative and the target date for starting on site. Contractors and some building industry professionals will argue strongly that a contractor should be appointed at the outset to set up the planning and conditions of sub-contract and that they can offer valuable buildability advice from conception. The employer, they say, cannot employ them early enough in a scheme. They will even organise the design team. The recently published *Construction Management Forum Report and Guidance* (published by Reading University Centre for Strategic Studies in Construction, 1991) advises appointing a construction manager who collaborates with the designers and is responsible for programming the trade contractor packages. To this end, the construction manager would be able to advise on which trade contractors to approach and whether it is possible for the designers to carry the design to the stage where trade contractors could give sensible competitive prices for completing the design and carrying out the construction. The construction manager should be able to advise on packages of work better than most designers. Moreover, the construction manager would then not be a 'contractor' but a 'professional' thus removing from it all the contractual risks. However, the author would advise that the contractor should not be appointed too early in the project if it has a long gestation period – seven months before start-on-site is a rule-of-thumb to work by. The reasons for this are:

☐ During the early weeks of the design stage the contractor simply adds another link in a communication chain at a time when the design team and employer need to work very closely together.

☐ Contractors are primarily concerned with programme sequence and methodology. This can interfere with the creativity of the design team if introduced too early in the project. The design/build commercial buildings of the sixties are poor testimony to the economic and functional criteria adopted by contractors in an era where they had charge of conceptual design.

☐ The contractor will have difficulty in providing and sustaining a first class team to work in a lengthy pre-contract stage as it will want to use its best resources elsewhere. Preconstruction work has substantially less profit than work in the construction stage. The latter stage attracts more lucrative fees related to turnover of building costs.

☐ Some advice may be obtained free from potential contractors, typically, a tower crane and plant scheme for a project or comment on a notional construction programme. The quid pro quo is to allow them to tender.

☐ Contractors' preconstruction services are not cheap: £40,000 a month (1989) is common on a major project. Just a planner and a quantity surveyor will cost a minimum of £2,500 per week (1989). Over, say, an 18 month design period this adds up to an expense that is hard to justify.

☐ Staff moves and workloads vary and no contractor can truly guarantee the make-up of its construction team more than seven months ahead of the start on site. Thus the choice of the contractor on the basis of the project team it intends to put on the site in a year's time is highly questionable.

☐ The combined experience of a good design team, the pqs and the employer's representative is often superior to the experience of a contractor's pre-contract team put on the job as an interim measure.

INCENTIVES FOR THE D&M CONTRACTOR

At the core of the procurement system is a mechanism which gives bonuses if the d&m contractor performs to budget and a penalty if it does not. The discipline of performing to budget automatically means keeping to programme. The mechanism provides for the employer and the contractor to share cost-savings and cost over-runs within a pre-set band. Figure 7 shows a simple way of sharing savings or over-runs equally. This particular share formula extends continously on either side of the target cost. Thus the contractor runs the risk of earning no fee if the target cost is exceeded by only six per cent. Conversely, the contractor can continue to earn higher fees the more it saves on project costs.

A number of steps which can be made to improve the mechanism can be seen in Figure 8. A target cost band can be introduced. It is unlikely that the target cost has been determined accurately and therefore the target cost band would be a better basis for assessment. It is suggested the band should be of the order of one per cent of the target cost.

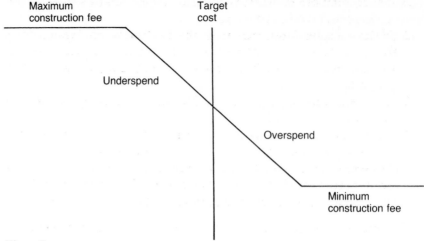

Figure 7

An upper limit and a lower limit on the construction and management fee can be introduced. The upper limit on the fee means that the employer knows the upper limit of the fee to be paid.

The formula can be adjusted to suit market conditions or can even be a subject of negotiation between employer and prospective contractors.

In some circumstances, it may be appropriate to place an upper limit on the prime costs which are to be paid by the employer; in effect giving a guaranteed maximum price for the contract. Adjustments to the target cost due to variations would also adjust the guaranteed maximum price.

D&M CONTRACTOR REQUEST FOR PROPOSAL

At the appropriate time the employer collates the documents which comprise the request for a proposal and sends them to, say, six contractors. The documents consist of the following items:

☐ A document outlining the system of procurement including the chosen target cost incentive mechanism.
☐ The outline specification updated to describe the scope of the work.
☐ The latest cost plan.
☐ A chart setting out the proposed overall contingencies and those for each package.

Max. construction
fee on prime cost

*Savings
60/40
in favour employer*

5%
target cost
band

Target fee

*Overspend
50/50 with employer*

Guaranteed maximum
price setting a ceiling
to the employer's cost

Figure 8: Target cost band introduced to the contractor's incentive mechanism

□ The programme showing procurement and notional construction activities in respect of packages.

□ Trade package documentation developed at the point of approaching the contractors including details of contracts placed (and their values) and the names of trade contractors being considered for other packages.

□ The explanatory memorandum and form of contract together with its appendices.

□ The explanatory memorandum and *Pro Forma Trade Contract* with details of performance bonds and parent company guarantees.

□ The proposed form of contract between contractor and trade contractor as agreed by architect and structural and services engineer.

□ Scheme design report and planning submittals.

The letter enclosing the request for proposal will ask contractors for:

□ A lump sum fee for pre-contract services and staff resources for this period against the given programme to be adjusted pro rata if the pre-contract period is extended. The cv's of the members of the contractor's team together with information showing the extent of their involvement in this preconstruction stage.

□ The basic fee to be applied to prime cost as set out in the *D&M Contractor's Agreement* during the construction stage. (Some people advocate obtaining a lump sum proposal for staff for pre-construction *and construction* services. The author prefers not to obtain a construction commitment to total staff resources until far more is known about the contract and in particular the strength and weaknesses of those trade contractors still to be selected.)

□ The maximum range of the sliding fee adjustment that is acceptable to the contractor on the basis of shared savings or overspending when calculating the difference between actual expenditure and the adjusted target cost. The adjusted target cost is of course the target cost as agreed at the time the contract is made, plus or minus the cost of any variations.

□ Adjustment, if any, and commitment to the schedule of contingencies to be used in assessment and agreement of the target cost.

□ A table indicating fixed weekly all-up costs including subsistence payments to each category of project personnel to be allocated to the construction stage of the project. Thus rates are to be fixed taking the programme, inflation and staff overtime into account.

□ A programme illustrating the deployment of personnel showing the proportion of time committed to the project:
  – In the construction stage (including mobilisation after the notice to proceed)
  – In the post contract stage to remedy defects and settle final accounts.
  – Names of key site-based personnel, their cv's, references and the proposed areas of their responsibility.

□ Confirmation that the contractor is prepared to work to the contract conditions and programme and adopt contracts with existing trade contractors and sub-consultants on the terms previously agreed with the employer.

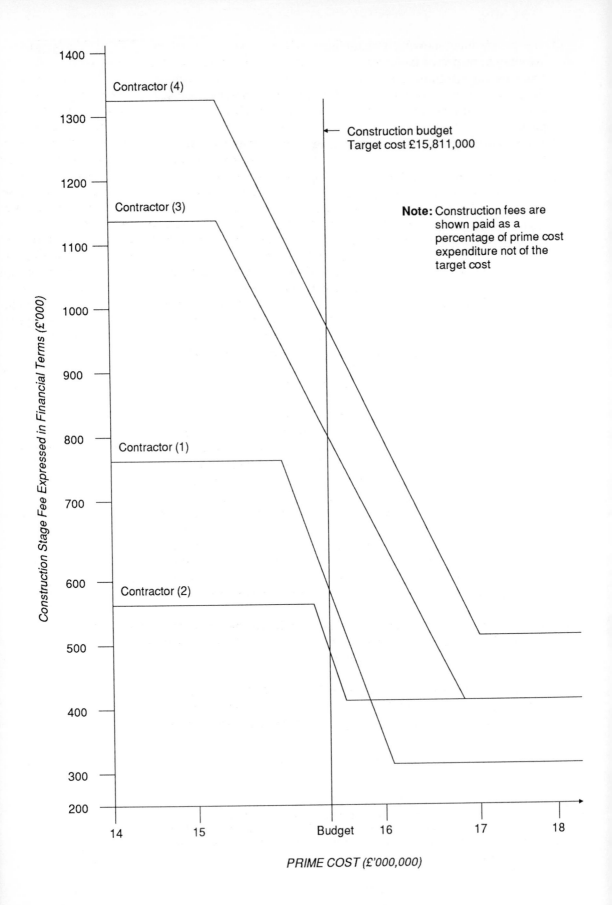

An analysis of the fee proposals and strength of teams put forward should result in a shortlist of two contractors. It is recommended that the widest range of fee offered should receive as much favour as the lowest base fee since this gives the incentive mechanism greatest strength. Thus the control of costs and the management of risk by the contractor will be rigorous, efficiency being rewarded and inefficiency punished. The effect on the out-turn costs resulting from different tender submissions received on a city fitting-out scheme using a target cost d&m contract can be seen in Figure 9. It shows how the contractor who offers the lowest base fee is not in this case prepared to accept risk in respect of his efficient performance earning a high bonus. Another contractor puts both base fee and incentive bonus high. Two other contractors who put the base fees at about the same level have very different ideas about the potential for an incentive. In the end, an interview of the two most favoured tenderers usually resolves the choice of contractor on the basis of people chemistry.

The two most favoured tenderers are requested to attend a design team meeting at which the employer's representative is present. The contractors are asked to bring the key staff members of their full-time site team including the project manager, the design co-ordinator, the planning manager, the services manager, the commercial manager and the site production manager. The head office director and sales staff should not be present.

The employer's representative then runs what is effectively site meeting No. 1. Each contractor explains its management structure and plans for site set-up. Programming and any design issues are discussed. Cost advice is sought and resources and logistics are discussed in as relaxed an atmosphere as possible. Telephones should be available for the team to consult back-up resources. A wide range of subjects is discussed including technical problems encountered by the design team and management and strategic decisions in respect of unlet packages. It is important to probe all the contractor's senior personnel on subjects close to their expertise and not to let one spokesperson dominate the discussions. The meetings will last two hours or more and should be lively working sessions which will help to establish rapport as well as testing leadership, experience and balance of the contractor's team.

In the author's experience one contractor's team will give the employer's design team substantially more 'comfort' than the other and the decision to employ that contractor is always unanimous.

THE D&M CONTRACTOR'S PRE-CONSTRUCTION DUTIES

The *D&M Contractor's Agreement* should include a complete list of duties to be performed in the pre-construction stage. The principal duties are listed below:

☐ Offer construction advice to the design team in respect of planning

Figure 9 (facing page): Typical tenders received on a target cost d&m contract. While contractor 2 offered the lowest base fee, it was not prepared to put much risk on the line in respect of incentive. Contractors 1 and 3 were interviewed in final assessment and contractor 1 was selected

and buildability with particular reference to labour and plant saving methods of assembly.

☐ Collaborate with the pqs in keeping to the detailed cost plan for construction work included in the *D&M Contractor's Agreement* and advise on the costs of developing the design so that the d&m contractor is party to the build-up of the target cost document.

☐ Prepare a fully detailed construction programme for the works having regard to dates agreed with trade contractors already appointed.

☐ Be party to the building up and assembly of the employer's requirements.

☐ Prepare package documentation for the 'non-design' and the site preliminaries packages. In collaboration with the pqs send out outstanding trade contract tender documents, conduct tender interviews (with the employer's representative, pqs and design team present) and make recommendations of selections to the employer's representative.

☐ Take over the management and supervision of mock-ups, off-site fabrication, including any testing.

☐ Carry out temporary works design to the structural consultant's approval and if appropriate, liaise with party wall surveyor and neighbouring properties.

☐ Agree costs of preliminaries to form part of the target cost and obtain estimates for connections by the public and statutory utilities.

☐ Progress trade contractors' outstanding shop drawings required for sanction and incorporation into the employer's requirements.

☐ Agree terms and appointment of the adjudicator for the construction stage.

☐ Agree provisional sums (if any) or budget estimates to be used in the target cost for work not let on the proposed date for the agreement of the target cost.

☐ Obtain all temporary licences and consents from statutory authorities to enable the works to proceed. Organise any site survey or site investigations work.

The design team led by the architect continues to work with the specialist trade contractors and develops the remaining tender packages in conjunction with the d&m contractor. The d&m contractor puts together the packages for preliminaries and the other packages which have not been tendered. The d&m contractor carries out the design of temporary works to be included in certain tender packages such as groundwork and sub-structure. The design team assembles the employer's requirements comprising consultants' drawings, specialist trade contractor drawings and a detailed specification. At the same time the cost plan is developed into the target cost document with pqs estimates being substituted by the actual tender prices. Approved variations to trade contractors' work resulting from design evolution are incorporated as is the agreed contingency (as published in the request for a proposal) for each package. The d&m contractor also supervises any off-site fabrication that may be taking place under a direct contract with the employer in order to meet the programme. The d&m contractor draws up a detailed construction programme taking into account any dates already agreed with trade contractors.

RELATIONSHIPS BETWEEN DESIGN AND TARGET COST

The relationship between extent of design and target cost and the level of detail to which the employer's requirements are developed depends largely on the time available for the design period and the extent to which the employer wishes to define the end product fully. There is no short cut to the level of information necessary in order to construct a building. It is a question of what is designed under the employer's control and what is to be designed under the d&m contractor's control. The system so far described assumes that on a large project, say in excess of £25m, all the major trade contractors are appointed in advance of the appointment of the d&m contractor. Thus the most influential trade contracts (say 80 per cent) are priced in a period of six to nine months inclusive of submittal and receipt of planning consent and tendering. The pre-contract period can be shortened with say 20 per cent of the work priced at the stage of agreeing the target cost but then the employer must accept higher contingencies to cover design development and a higher negotiated target cost. The employer would also have less control on the detail of the end product which would rely on performance specifications rather than developed design solutions approved by the employer.

The author's one experience of trying to impose a target cost after the notice to proceed was issued and construction well under way, was a failure. The contractor, who was in a secure position would not agree the contingency figure in respect of risk at an amount that the employer and pqs thought was reasonable. The employer preferred to take the risk itself and pay a flat management fee. So the notion was abandoned. The conclusion is that unless the target cost is agreed the notice to proceed should be withheld by the employer. If the employer cannot agree the target cost with a contractor then it is, of course, able to enter into negotiations with another contractor.

THE SPECIFICATION

The specification must be written by the design consultants (and personally by the individual responsible for each part of the design). It is the document that controls the construction stage. It will be referred to frequently to decide what constitutes a change in the employer's requirements thus giving rise to a variation order and therefore an adjustment to the target cost. It must be complete, clear and unambiguous. It must define all the design undertaken by the consultants and shown on their drawings. It should also define all the trade contract work that has been let or has still to be designed in the construction stage. It should clearly specify all the requirements which the employer wishes to impose upon the outstanding design that is to be undertaken by the contractor. This may include the use of schedules and performance criteria. All aspects of the outline specification agreed at the end of Stage 2 should be addressed and checked. Access for maintenance, cost in use and performance requirements should be set out precisely. Samples, testing procedures and mock-ups should be defined. If it is thought that a tenant may want its own contractors on site before practical completion then the specification has to set out the ground rules for co-existence in the form of an access regime and schedule of facilities to be provided by the contractor to the tenant's contractors and designers.

National Building Specifications are a good starting point in defining quality, but must be bespoke to the project in question. Handover and commissioning procedures should be set out in detail together with arrangements for fuel, power and use of permanent lights. Some of these matters will have already been addressed in the trade contracts. If there are items of equipment directly supplied by the employer which require transporting, handling and installing they should be listed in detail and responsibilities defined.

The employer should stipulate those items on which it wishes to preserve a right of approval such as lift car finishes or choice of veneer in meeting rooms.

The following items should be addressed when drawing up the specification of each package:

- ☐ General description.
- ☐ Phasing, programme constraints, site access arrangements.
- ☐ Agreements made with third parties in respect of construction and methodology.
- ☐ Site facilities for the employer's representative, pqs and inspectorate.
- ☐ Insurance requirements particularly in respect of sprinklers, window cradles, lifts and pressure vessels.
- ☐ Existing survey and ground investigation reports.
- ☐ Responsibilities in payments to statutory utilities, building control fees and other third parties.
- ☐ Special requirements of the employer's representative to sanction calculations, literature, samples or design.
- ☐ Distribution and magnitude of loads to be assumed and any other design data essential to the contractor to complete the design.
- ☐ Life cycle requirements, studies and recommendations to be adopted.
- ☐ Special marketing or institutional requirements to be safeguarded while detailing design (e.g. nett lettable sq ft of office space).
- ☐ Copies of statutory consents, waivers and agreements made at the point of publication of the employer's requirements.

☐ Obligations on the d&m contractor during the defects period and constraints if the building is occupied.

☐ Records to be kept by the d&m contractor and reporting procedures.

☐ Meetings to be attended by the d&m contractor.

☐ Variation procedure.

DRAWINGS AND SCHEDULES

The drawings and schedules prepared by the design consultants and trade contractors are assembled as part of the documentation of the employer's requirements.

On a major project this could amount to 400 consultants' drawings and some 800 trade contractors' drawings. There is something to be said for reducing all drawing material required for the legal documentation to A3 and A4. It makes duplication and reference easier to handle.

BUILDING CONTROL

It is imperative that the public utilities, building control officers and the fire officer are properly consulted with agreements fully documented and incorporated in the employer requirements. Any change under this procurement system puts the employer at risk.

AGREEMENT OF THE TARGET COST AND NOTICE TO PROCEED

Before the start of site construction it is necessary for the employer and the d&m contractor to reach agreement on the target cost so that the notice to proceed can be given.

The target cost will include pqs/contractor estimates of all packages of work not yet priced plus the agreed build up of costs for trade contracts already let, contractor's staff and site preliminaries. The target cost must make allowance for day-works included in packages which the d&m contractor will control and the contingency factors agreed when the contractor was selected. Provisional sums can be included which upon resolution would mean adjustment to the target cost. However they should be avoided if possible or at least limited. Negotiations must ensure that the target cost does not include hidden contingencies which allow the d&m contractor to readily achieve an increased fee when they are not spent.

Once agreed the target cost will only be adjusted to take into account changes to the employer's requirements.

Having reached agreement on the target cost and having approved the employer's requirements, the employer issues the notice to proceed and the employer's consultants switch to become the d&m contractor's sub-consultants. This is effected by engrossment of the agreement between contractor and consultant.

KEEPING TRACK OF THE TARGET COST

While it is the architect's role to assemble all the information comprising the employer's requirements, it is the responsibility of the pqs to keep an up-to-date record of costs by constantly replacing initial estimates with hard figures based on quotations from the trade contractors and the d&m contractor. The record lists the daywork and elemental cost content of every package whether it is estimated or priced. Contingencies already agreed at the request for a proposal stage are allocated to each package and an overall contingency of two per cent added on top. This can be seen in Table 7. The contractor's design management fee and construction stage design fees are added to the package costs to create the target cost.

NEGOTIATION

If the pqs and the d&m contractor are working well together negotiation is a mathematical exercise and a formality. Both parties have been party to the cost build up and fees and contingencies have been agreed at the outset. The amounts put in for preliminaries which are not covered by lump sum quotes such as electricity, water, drawing reproduction, telephones, computers, general service gangs and general scaffolding might be an area of disagreement. The d&m contractor and pqs will both have records to fall back on and the margin of disagreement produces a sum of money that is fairly insignificant in the totality of the whole scheme. However, there needs to be a meeting, say, six weeks before starting on site, chaired by the employer's representative to agree the employer's requirements, the construction programme and target cost. These are appended to the contract and must be included before the notice to proceed can be given.

NOTICE TO PROCEED

The employer issues the notice to proceed when he is entirely happy with the terms of the contract. At the same time the appointment of the adjudicator must be ratified and insurances put into place. The consultants

Table 7: Example of build up of target cost

TARROW HOUSE FITTING OUT (SHEET 4)

Provisional target cost statement (issue 1) as at 23.12.89

Pkge No.	Package name	Trade contractor	Pqs budget cost inc. inflation allowance £	Trade contr. tender inc. prem. time inflation allow. £	Prov. assess. for work not costed £	Prov. sum for work not incl. £	Package/ daywork contingency £	Overall contingency 2% £	Target cost £	Contractual adds. to target cost £	Adjusted target cost £	Antic. final prime cost £
7577	Trading desks	Cost plan 4/4A	874,300	Nil	817,103	Nil	40,855	16,342	874,300	Nil	874,300	874,300
7615	Doors	Cost plan 4/4A	89,900	Nil	94,000	Nil	4,700	1,880	100,580	Nil	100,580	100,580
7700	Decorations	David James	161,600	69,451	20,000	25,000	5,723	2,289	122,463	Nil	122,463	122,463
7810	Intl. signs	Cost plan 4/4A	27,700	Nil	25,000	Nil	1,250	500	26,750	Nil	26,750	26,750
7830	Blinds	Doreen Blinds	110,900	46,143	Nil	Nil	2,307	923	49,373	Nil	49,373	49,373
8000	Mock-up	Cost plan 4/4A	25,000	Nil	Nil	Nil	Nil	Nil	Nil	Nil	Nil	Nil
9000	Premium time	Cost plan 4/4A	700,000	Nil	Nil	Nil	Nil	Nil	Nil	Nil	Nil	Nil
	Sub-total A		12,496,300	5,563,261	5,959,859	502,317	525,876	210,350	12,901,663	Nil	12,901,663	12,901,662
	Con. stage fee d&m contractor (3.5%)		437,371	194,714	208,595	17,581	18,406	7,362	451,558	Nil	451,558	451,558
	Sub-total B		12,933,671	5,757,975	6,168,454	519,898	544,281	217,713	13,353,221	Nil	13,353,221	13,353,220
9775	Screen based furn. Client est.		536,000	Nil	Nil	536,000	Nil	Nil	536,000	Nil	536,000	536,000
	d&m contractor fee on furn. (3.5%)		18,760	Nil	Nil	18,760	Nil	Nil	18,760	Nil	18,760	18,760
	Sub-total C		13,488,431	5,757,975	6,168,454	1,074,658	544,281	217,713	13,907,981	Nil	13,907,981	13,907,980
	Architect's fee (3% of sub-total B)		388,010	172,739	185,054	15,597	16,328	6,531	400,597	Nil	400,597	400,597
	Serv. engs. fee (1.5% of sub-total B)		194,005	86,370	92,527	7,798	8,164	3,266	200,298	Nil	200,298	200,298
	GRAND TOTAL		14,070,446	6,017,084	6,446,034	1,098,054	568,774	227,510	14,508,876	Nil	14,508,876	14,508,876

switch to becoming sub-consultants to the d&m contractor. The employer's contracts with the trade contractors are novated to the d&m contractor and the d&m contractor is immediately entitled to a fee on the prime cost of all goods that have been manufactured and paid for to date. This alone acts as a catalyst to agreement and speedy signing up of documentation by both contractor and sub-consultants. The contractor mobilises in order to start work on site.

TARGET COST ADJUSTMENT
Reasons for adjusting the target cost and the mechanism for doing it are set out in Stage 7. However, it should be understood that while all contractor outgoings in respect of prime cost are reimbursed on a refundable basis, not all variations in respect of trade contracts cause the target cost to be adjusted. The risks which the contractor controls on behalf of the employer should be covered by provision of contingency sums in each package plus a overall contingency of two per cent. In effect it is the control of the contingency money which will lead to an increase or decrease of fee at the end of the project.

The employer's representative will administer the contract. On a large project he/she will be resident on site and in any case must be available on a full time basis. By delegation the pqs will look after valuation and matters to do with costs and payment. On a large project resident engineers will be appointed by the employer to oversee and inspect the structural work and installation of the building services. A site architect will inspect all architectural aspects of the works to ensure that they meet the employer's requirements. The team as a whole will sanction any outstanding design put forward by the contractor. This phrase 'sanctioned' is drawn from The BPF Manual and is used to denote that the designs carried out by the design-build contractor or trade contractors meet the employer's requirements. It does not imply any legal responsibility for those designs. An adjudicator is appointed when the contract is let to resolve any disputes quickly.

THE CONTRACT

The *D&M Contractor's Agreement* provides the legal framework for the d&m contractor to:

☐ Manage the work and utilise the resources paid for by the employer in the most efficient manner.

☐ Assist the employer by using its knowledge of the construction industry and its commercial skills.

☐ Collaborate with the employer and design consultants to meet or improve on the agreed quality, time and cost targets for the project. This is achieved by offering the d&m contractor a reasonably attainable opportunity to earn a fee substantially higher than the level of fees normally achieved on a standard cost reimbursable contract. The d&m contractor is encouraged to employ its most able managers on the project. They are reinforced by the design team which has experience and knowledge of the job going back to its very inception. The penalty of underachieving normal levels of management fees provides further incentive for the d&m contractor to perform.

As the d&m contractor takes responsibility for the design consultants it cannot claim that its performance has been regulated by matters outside its control – namely a sub-standard or restricted flow of design information.

ADJUSTMENT TO THE TARGET COST

To maintain the d&m contractor's incentive, the target cost needs to be adjusted throughout the construction stage of the project to account for:

☐ Variations to the scope of work as expressed in the employer's requirements.

☐ The resolution of provisional sums if included in the target cost.

☐ The cost of certain defined risks retained by the employer, such as changes in statutory requirements or delays in the handover of the site.

☐ The granting of extensions of time in respect of the above reasons thereby generating prolongation costs.

☐ The employer accelerating any part or all of the works.

The target cost should be adjusted as soon as possible after a variation order is issued. In practice, however, trade contractors and their sub-contractors are tediously slow at responding to price information. The adjusted target cost should be published monthly with estimated figures in brackets to be removed when hard figures are agreed with trade contractors and the d&m contractor.

EXTENSIONS TO TRADE CONTRACTS
Trade contractors are entitled to an extension of their trade contract period if delays occur for the following reasons:

- ☐ 'Force majeure' (but not shortages of materials or labour).
- ☐ Loss or damage by fire.
- ☐ Variation instructed by the employer's representative if proved to affect the trade contractor's completion date.
- ☐ Statutory authority changes of public utilities work which delay the trade contracts.
- ☐ Late receipt of information or instructions.
- ☐ Failure to provide access to the trade contract works on the agreed date.
- ☐ Opening up of works which prove to be in good order.
- ☐ Other parties who through reasonably unforeseeable circumstances delay the trade contractor's work.
- ☐ Change in legislation.

CONTRACTOR SAVINGS
Apart from savings from the control of the contingencies built into the target cost totalling some five to seven per cent, a chance exists after agreement of the target cost for the d&m contractor to 'value engineer' the work. The contractor can carry out a value engineering exercise on those packages which are not yet let in a similar way to that carried out by the employer as described on page 19.

As the target cost under these circumstances remains unaltered, the d&m contractor is encouraged to search for cost reductions although it will be sharing savings within the pre-agreed band with the employer. Any changes to the specification that lead to savings will need the approval of the employer's representative to ensure that the employer's requirements are still met.

PRELIMINARIES
The other opportunity for saving is the efficient control of expenditure in respect of site preliminaries which in traditional management contracts is considered by many critics to be a notorious area of extravagance. Extra expenditure on any part of the preliminaries has to be agreed by the employer's representative and although it will be reimbursed as prime cost it does not result in the target cost being adjusted unless the expenditure is directly caused by a variation. For this reason preliminaries should be well defined before their inclusion into the target cost.

INCENTIVES FOR DESIGN CONSULTANTS
Some professionals take the view that they will always give their best endeavours and it is unprofessional to accept incentives of any kind for doing their job. Other professionals will not accept bonus payments from

a developer but are willing to share in the financial success of a contractor's scheme. The work of designers during the construction phase of the project involves very little pure design and mainly entails production of detail drawings and clarification of clashes and design intent. It also involves the co-ordination and approval of outstanding shop drawings from trade contractors. The author does not believe that it is necessary to offer incentives to the consultants. However, if the d&m contractor insists that it is essential, there is no harm in setting up an incentive scheme. Few consultants are likely to accept a penalty of reduced fees without raising their basic fee in the first place to cover that risk.

INCENTIVES FOR CONTRACTOR'S STAFF

The physical work on site is entirely carried out by the trade contractors. The d&m contractor creates the management framework and environment within which the trade contractors can perform efficiently. The successful construction of the project depends upon the speed and quality of the trade contractors' work. Therefore the selection of the right contractor is vital as is the quality and commitment of its individuals. The target cost mechanism gives a golden opportunity for the contracting industry to initiate an incentive mechanism for individuals. Staff could be rewarded directly with a proportion of the bonus acquired by the contractor. In the long term this might go a long way to attracting a higher calibre of individual into the construction industry.

CONTRACT ADMINISTRATION

The amount of paperwork generated between d&m contractor and the employer's representative is substantially less than for other forms of contract as there is less reason to document everything in pursuit of claims. Similarly, paperwork exchanges between d&m contractor and design consultants are substantially reduced because weekly meetings ensure early clarification of difficulties. There is less reason to record everything that takes place between designer and contractor when the designer is part of the contractor's internal project organisation.

The volume of correspondence and notices exchanged between the contractor and the trade contractors will be comparable with that on standard management contracts. Claims however will not be a 'soft touch' since the d&m contractor will not want to reduce its potential bonus. Where contra-charging is appropriate it will be vigorously enforced.

Regular meetings between the d&m contractor's commercial manager and the pqs are necessary with the occasional attendance of the employer's representative to review outstanding cost information and agree revisions to the target cost occasioned by variations. The employer's representative and the d&m contractor's project manager need to meet weekly on an informal basis to progress cost information, actions by third parties and outstanding instructions or correspondence and discuss current or forthcoming problems.

Monthly site meetings chaired by the employer's representative, to discuss and record progress reports and resources provide a formal record of the project. They also keep the principals of the firms involved in touch with the true state of the project – not least the employer.

THE ADJUDICATOR

The principal reason for having an adjudicator is to resolve disputes quickly rather than allowing them to fester, so that all parties know where they stand with some certainty. The adjudicator, who is paid a retainer by the employer but is employed hourly in respect of time investigations disputes, is provided with notes of all site meetings and makes regular visits to the site regardless of whether there is a dispute or not. The adjudicator has private meetings with both the employer's representative and the d&m contractor's project manager. Thus at all times he/she has a good knowledge of how the job is progressing. The adjudicator is given authority to settle disputes between the employer and the contractor in respect of:

☐ Extensions of time.
☐ Certification of items of prime cost.
☐ Adjustments to the target cost.
☐ Either party's entitlement to terminate the d&m contractor's appointment.

He/she also has similar authority to rule in disputes between the d&m contractor and any trade contractor. The adjudicator's role finishes at practical completion. Until then his/her decisions are binding.

After practical completion previous decisions by the adjudicator can be referred to the High Court.

When a dispute arises the adjudicator is presented with submissions from both parties. Only one subject at a time can be submitted and claims for extensions of time must be separated from claims for costs. The adjudicator has seven days to examine the submission and using the technique of 'pendulum arbitration' must not compromise but rule in favour of one party or the other. The loser bears the cost of the adjudicator's additional hourly fees charged which are not reclaimable as prime cost. Pendulum arbitration forces both parties to be reasonable and consider the other's point of view. It controls exaggerated levels of claim and levels of expectancy which accompany submissions. Under this system most claims get sorted out without recourse to the adjudicator albeit outside the door.

SANCTION OF CONTRACTOR'S DESIGN

Contractually the employer's representative has the right to sanction the d&m contractor's design and outstanding trade design for conformity with the employer's requirements. The architect appointed to carry out the design up to the point of letting the contract will normally be sub-consultant to the d&m contractor. Thus sanction of drawings will only be necessary if there is some doubt in the contractor's mind as to whether or not its intended proposals are within the contract specifications. The d&m contractor has the responsibility of seeking all necessary statutory approvals to its design. The mechanical and electrical working drawings if prepared by contractors will need to be sanctioned by the services consultant working under the employer's representative as part of the inspectorate.

SITE INSPECTION

Inspectors are appointed to inspect the works to confirm that they meet the employer's requirements. The inspectors' role can be performed by the design consultants operating on a 'Chinese wall' principle whereby the department responsible for the inspectorate for the employer is separate from the department responsible for the design under the contractor. This only works where personnel are dedicated to inspectorate duties and these individuals are clearly different from those completing the design for the d&m contractor. This has the advantage of continuity but the drawback of occasional conflict of interest. If the employer wishes to introduce changes to the scheme, this principle gives it direct access to the design consultants. Alternatively a firm of building surveyors may take on the inspectorate role. The inspectorate is answerable and reports to the employer's representative.

ACCELERATION AND BONUS INCENTIVES TO TRADE CONTRACTORS

The contractor may, with the approval of the employer's representative, set up incentive payments for trade contractors for attaining set target dates. Such incentive payments, while considered part of the prime cost, would not normally cause adjustments to the target cost. However if the employer decides to issue an instruction to increase the pace of work to certain packages by means of acceleration, any additional costs would be treated as a variation.

For acceleration agreements to work the trade contractor must see that the basic costs of increasing resources will be re-imbursed whatever the results and that additionally, there is an incentive reward to increase its profit. They can be made to work, particularly if geared toward weekly output. Thus if the first date is not met, opportunities still exist to increase margins. If properly thought out they are also a useful means of expunging all existing claims and starting afresh on packages that for one reason or another have got behind the programme.

VALUATION AND PAYMENT

From time to time the employer's representative will require proof from the d&m contractor that trade contractors have been paid for interim certificates before issuing a further interim certificate. The d&m contractor is obliged to pay the relevant trade contractor within 21 days of each certificate issued by the pqs having been certified by the employer's representative.

The employer pays the d&m contractor's prime cost, less retention and the construction stage basic management fee on a monthly basis following the d&m contractor's submission and pqs agreement of valuations. Prime costs include such items as the design consultants' disbursements, the design fee, the d&m contractor's staff and labour, and the cost of materials, plant, consumable stores and services provided by the contractor including fuel and insurance. The amounts payable by the d&m contractor to trade contractors form the 'lion's share' of the total payment and are paid after deducting discounts and any amounts to be recovered from trade contractors because trade contractors have defaulted, e.g. produced unsatisfactory work.

The employer is not obliged to pay what in the employer's representative's opinion are excessive unreasonable costs or costs resulting from negligence.

VARIATION ORDER REQUEST TO A TRADE CONTRACT

ORIGINATOR'S
SECTION

Originator's Name:

Tel. No:

Company:

Date of request:

Trade Contractor(s)
involved:

Originator's assessment - grade value [ ]   (see opposite)

- reason for request

- other reason

Documents accompanying request:

Instruction required

CONTRACT ADMINISTRATION SECTION

Comment (if any) on originator's assessment:

Action taken:

Instruction No.   Date Issued

AUTHORISATION SECTION

	Authority	Signature
Grade X	DMC	
Y	Emp. Rep.	
Z	Emp.	

Copies to:

GUIDE NOTES

Grades of Expenditure

X	Under £2000
Y	£2001 - £25000
Z	Over £25000

Instruction which in the opinion of the Originator will alter
the price - REASON

A Design omission in the Trade Contract documents

B Improvement resulting from subcontract design

C Forced upon project from shop drawing co-ordination

D New information on existing site conditions

E Employer has changed his requirements

F Improvement in development value

G Cost saving

H Saving in tenant fitting out or running costs

I Programme advantage or insurance

J Statutory body requirement

K Public utility requirement come to light since placing of
trade contract

Figure 10: Variation order request to a trade contract

The employer will pay the amount due less retention within 14 days after the date of the interim certificate.

Materials and goods not yet delivered to site can be included with the consent of the employer's representative and subject to transference of ownership and certificates of indemnity being signed.

RETENTION

Half the retention is released on practical completion and half upon agreement of the final certificate.

VARIATION PROCEDURE

Any party involved in the project can raise a variation request on the form shown in Figure 10. This form specifically relates to the trade contracts and is examined at the weekly meeting between the d&m contractor and employer's representative. It is up to the employer's representative whether or not the request is agreed and whether or not it constitutes a variation to the main contract. No variation order is issued without some estimate of price being provided by the contractor, albeit broad brush to be firmed up when hard costs come in from the trade contractors involved.

ADJUSTMENT OF FEES AND FINAL ACCOUNTS

At practical completion the likely 'actual' out-turn costs of construction need to be established and an adjustment takes place to fees paid to the contractor on the basis of the incentive mechanism formula. This is fine tuned to a precise figure prior to the release of the final certificate.

THE FORMULA

The mechanism for calculating the fees due is shown in Figure 11. It has been assumed in this particular formula that any savings or excess-expenditure is divided equally between the employer and the d&m contractor within pre-set parameters. As pointed out in Stage 4, arrangements for sharing may be varied.

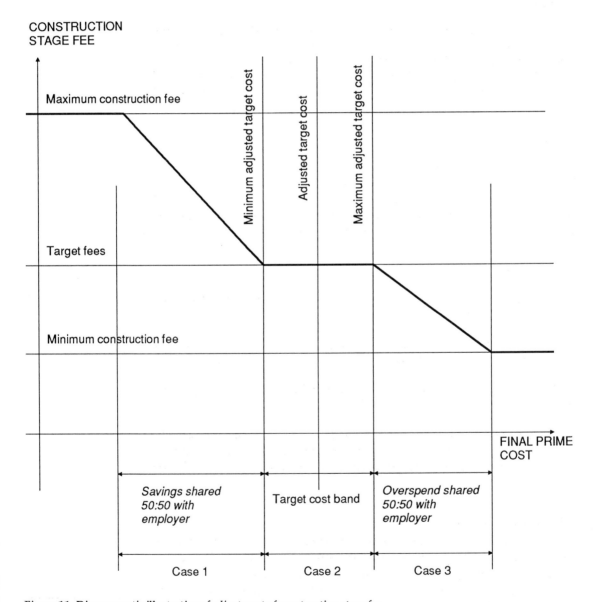

Figure 11: Diagrammatic illustration of adjustment of construction stage fee

CASE 1

If the final prime cost is less than the adjusted minimum target cost the construction fee will consist of the target (basic) fee plus the difference between the final prime cost and the adjusted minimum target cost expressed as a percentage of the adjusted minimum target cost and divided by two. This is subject to a maximum construction stage fee of R per cent of the adjusted target cost.

CASE 2

If the final prime cost falls within the target cost band the construction fee will be the target fee.

CASE 3

If the final prime cost exceeds the adjusted maximum target cost the construction fee will consist of the target basic fee minus the difference between the final prime cost and the adjusted maximum target cost expressed as a percentage of the adjusted maximum target cost and divided by two. This is subject to a minimum construction stage fee of Q per cent of the adjusted target cost.

RANGE OF RATES

The total range of possible rates for the construction stage fee will accordingly be Q per cent to R per cent and any overspend greater than R per cent of the adjusted target cost or underspend of less than Q per cent of the adjusted target cost will have no financial implications on the minimum of maximum rates of the construction fee.

DEFINITIONS

(Adjusted) target cost band: The (adjusted) target cost plus or minus X per cent of the (adjusted) target cost.

(Adjusted) minimum target cost: The (adjusted) target cost minus X per cent of the (adjusted) target cost.

(Adjusted) maximum target cost: The (adjusted) target cost plus X per cent of the (adjusted) target cost.

The purpose of the target cost band is to save argument on pricing everything to the nearest penny and it recognises that estimating is not an exact science. The author recommends the band should be set at plus or minus ½ per cent.

FINAL ACCOUNTS

Upon completion of the defects period and settlement of final accounts the same calculation takes place on finalised figures prior to all retention being released. The sums of money in retention funds are such as to outweigh the sums of money owed by the d&m contractor to the employer in the event of a downward adjustment.

Appendix 1: Model architect's agreement

Dated ....

[Employer] and [Architect]

Architect's Agreement relating to ....

ARCHITECT'S AGREEMENT

CONTENTS

THIS AGREEMENT is made on ....

BETWEEN

1. [.................................] whose registered office is at [....] ("the Employer");

and

2. The partners in [.............................] (being the persons listed in the [Eighth] Schedule) of/[.................................]
LIMITED whose registered office is at [............................]
("the Architect").

RECITALS

(A) The Employer intends to proceed with [the demolition of the existing building,] the design and construction of [...........................]
("the Basic Works") and, if the Employer so elects, the design and construction therein of Fitting-Out Works (as defined below) (together called "the Works") at [....]
("the Site") as more particularly described in the Brief.

(B) The Works are to be carried out in two stages, namely the Pre-Construction Stage and the Construction Stage (as defined below), and at the date hereof the Works are in the Pre-Construction Stage.

(C) The Employer wishes to appoint the Architect as architect to perform the Pre-Construction Services, the Construction Services and the Additional Services, if any, on the terms and conditions set out in this Agreement.

(D) The Employer wishes to engage the D&M Contractor (as defined below) upon the provisions of a Design and Management Agreement ("the D&M Contract") to provide advice and assistance in the planning, organisation and programming of the Works and to advise on the outline design for the Works during the Pre-Construction Stage and, if instructed by the Employer, to complete or procure the completion of the detailed design of the Works and to procure, manage, organise and continually supervise the construction of the Works during the Construction Stage.

(E) The Employer intends to let the whole of the completed development either as a single demise or as separate demises to a person or persons as yet undetermined ("Tenants").

(F) The Client has relied and will continue to rely upon the Architect's skill and judgment in respect of all matters covered by this Agreement.

NOW IT IS HEREBY AGREED as follows:-

1. DEFINITIONS

1.1 In this Agreement expressions defined in the Recitals hereto shall have the meanings therein given, and the following expressions shall have the following meanings:-

"Additional Services" has the meaning set out in clause 4.1;

"Anticipated Target Cost" means the detailed initial estimate of the Target Cost included in the Brief;

"Brief" means the document set out in Part A of the Fifth Schedule containing, inter alia, the Pre-Construction Programme in detail, the Construction Programme in outline and the Budget;

"Budget" means (during the Pre-Construction Stage) the price breakdown of the Anticipated Target Cost included in the Brief and (during the Construction Stage) the price breakdown of the Target Cost or (if it has been adjusted pursuant to the D&M Contract) the Adjusted Target Cost or, where appropriate in both cases, any such price breakdown as updated from time to time by the Employer's Representative;

"Construction Programme" means the detailed programme for the design and construction of the Basic Works during the Construction Stage to be prepared and agreed by the D&M Contractor under the D&M Contract in consultation and co-operation with the Professional Team and includes any further such programme or programmes in respect of any Fitting-Out Works (which shall be prepared and agreed on the same basis) or, where appropriate, any such programme as updated from time to time in accordance with the D&M Contract;

"Construction Services" means the services referred to in clause 3.2 and in Part B of the Second Schedule;

"Construction Stage" means the second phase of the Works involving the completion of the detailed design of the Works in accordance with the Employer's Requirements and the carrying-out and completion of the construction of the Works on Site (including any remedial works or other works or services after practical completion of the Works);

"D&M Contractor" means the contractor to be engaged by the Employer upon the provisions of the D&M Contract or any further or other such contractor for the time being engaged by the Employer to provide any of the advice, assistance and other activities referred to in Recital D;

"D&M Contractor's Appointment" has the meaning set out in clause 12.1;

"Day" means and includes Monday to Sunday but excludes statutory bank holidays unless otherwise specified;

"Design Information" has the meaning set out in clause 13.1;

"Employer's Representative" means the person named as such in Paragraph A of the First Schedule or, in the event of the person so named ceasing to act for any reason, such other person as the Employer shall nominate for that purpose (after consultation with the Architect), provided that references to the Employer's Representative shall be deemed to be references to the Employer's Representative and/or any person to whom the Employer's Representative may, with the prior consent of the Employer, delegate any of his powers, duties or responsibilities (including, without limitation, any quantity surveyor carrying out any fiscal or measurement function so delegated);

"Employer's Requirements" means the Brief, together with the designs, specifications and descriptions of any other requirements in respect of the Basic Works to be prepared by the Professional Team with the assistance of the D&M Contractor during the Pre-Construction Stage on the basis of the Brief and inserted as Part B of the Fifth Schedule prior to commencement of the Construction Stage, and includes, where appropriate, any further such designs, specifications and descriptions which may be prepared by the Professional Team (or issued by Tenants and adopted by the Employer) in respect of any Fitting-Out Works. For the avoidance of doubt, any requirements of such designs, specifications or descriptions forming part of the Employer's Requirements for the Basic Works which are not referable or applicable exclusively to the Basic Works shall be considered to apply to the whole of the Works, subject to anything expressly to the contrary or inconsistent therewith contained in any such designs, specifications or descriptions;

"Final Prime Cost" has the meaning set out in the D&M Contract;

"Fitting-Out Works" means any works of fitting-out or partial fitting-out in addition to the Basic Works;

"Pre-Construction Programme" means the programme for the general performance of the services of the Professional Team and the D&M Contractor during the Pre-Construction Stage prepared by the Employer's Representative and included in the Brief or, where appropriate, such programme as updated from time to time by the Employer's Representative;

"Pre-Construction Services" means the services referred to in clauses 3.1 and 3.2 and in Part A of the Second Schedule;

"Pre-Construction Stage" means the initial phase of the Works involving the provision of advice and assistance in the planning, organisation and programming of the Works, the preparation of an outline design for the Works and the preparation of the Employer's Requirements, the Construction Programme and the Target Cost;

"Pre-Ordered Trade Contract Packages" means those works and other activities to be carried out and/or materials to be supplied as part of the Works by trade contractors under trade contracts placed by the Employer during the Pre-Construction Stage, all of which are to be novated by the Employer to the D&M Contractor during the Construction Stage;

"Professional Team" means the consultants set out in Paragraph A of the First Schedule and any further or other consultants from time to time appointed by the Employer in connection with the Works;

"Target Cost" and "Adjusted Target Cost" have the respective meanings set out in the D&M Contract.

1.2 References in this Agreement to statutory or regulatory provisions shall be construed as references to those provisions as respectively amended or re-enacted from time to time (whether before or after the date of this Agreement) and shall include any provisions of which they are re-enactments (with or without modifications) and any subordinate legislation made under such provisions.

2. APPOINTMENT

2.1 The Employer hereby appoints the Architect, and the Architect hereby agrees to carry out and complete the Pre-Construction Services, the Construction Services and the Additional Services, if any, fully and faithfully in the best interests of the Employer in accordance with the instructions of the Employer's Representative and upon the terms and conditions set out in this Agreement.

2.2 The appointment of the Architect shall be deemed to have commenced with effect from the date upon which the Architect shall have begun to perform the services to be performed hereunder.

3. ARCHITECT'S OBLIGATIONS

3.1 As part of the Pre-Construction Services, the Architect shall:-

3.1.1 advise, assist and co-operate with the Employer, the Employer's Representative, the other members of the Professional Team and the D&M Contractor in the planning and cost estimating of and the organisation of preparations for the building works to be carried out and completed during the Construction Stage, and specifically to advise and assist such persons in drawing up the Employer's Requirements, the Construction Programme and the Target Cost;

3.1.2 examine the designs prepared or to be prepared by the other members of the Professional Team for compliance with the designs prepared or to be prepared by the Architect and, insofar as they relate to or affect the Architect's designs, with the Brief and the instructions and reasonable requirements of the Employer, and co-ordinate and integrate all such designs into the overall design for the Works;

3.1.3 examine the designs prepared or to be prepared pursuant to Pre-Ordered Trade Contract Packages for compliance with the designs prepared or to be prepared by the Architect and, insofar as they relate to or affect the Architect's designs, with the Brief and the instructions and reasonable requirements of the Employer, and co-ordinate and integrate all such designs into the overall design for the Works;

3.1.4 inspect at appropriate intervals (with the consent of the Employer's Representative) or when requested by the Employer's Representative the progress and quality of the works being executed pursuant to Pre-Ordered Trade Contract Packages to determine whether they are being executed in accordance with the appropriate contract documents; and

3.1.5 assist the Employer's Representative in co- ordinating the services to be performed by the other members of the Professional Team and securing the timely and proper performance of all such services.

3.2 As part of both the Pre-Construction Services and the Construction Services, the Architect shall:-

3.2.1 generally oversee and advise the Employer and the Employer's Representative upon all aspects of the Works insofar as they relate to the design of the Works prepared or to be prepared by or which are otherwise the responsibility of the Architect (whether under this Agreement or the D&M Contractor's Appointment);

3.2.2 advise the Employer's Representative on the Employer's Requirements (including the interpretation thereof) and upon the designs, details and specifications for and the time and cost implications of variations and proposed variations to the Employer's Requirements;

3.2.3 perform such of the Employer's Representative's powers, duties or responsibilities in relation to the administration of the Pre-Ordered Trade Contract Packages and the D&M Contract as the Employer's Representative shall delegate to him with the prior consent of the Employer, provided that such delegated services fall within the scope of the Architect's professional discipline;

3.2.4 carry out such further design and value engineering services as may be requested by the Employer's Representative in order to achieve economies required by the Employer;

3.2.5 provide all advice, drawings, information, documents, consents, comments, approvals, details, specifications, instructions and directions required from the Architect in connection with the Works promptly, efficiently and in good time so as not to delay or disrupt the progress of the Works; and

3.2.6 provide the Employer, the Employer's Representative, the other members of the Professional Team and the D&M Contractor upon request with such copies of all drawings, reports, details, specifications and other information in respect of the Works which have been prepared or used by the Architect as they may reasonably require.

3.3 The Architect shall proceed regularly and diligently with all the services to be provided by him hereunder in accordance with the timing requirements set out in the Pre-Construction Programme and the Construction Programme and without delaying or disrupting the services and the works to be carried out by others in consequence of any negligence, default or breach of contract on the part of the Architect. The Architect shall constantly use his best endeavours to prevent any delay or disruption to the progress of the Works and shall increase resources as necessary at his own expense in order to minimise any delays which become apparent.

3.4 The Architect shall at all times keep the Employer and the Employer's Representative fully informed and shall provide them with regular reports on all matters of interest to a prudent client, together with all such other information in regard to the Works as the Employer and the Employer's Representative may require. In addition, the Architect shall, as and when requested to do so by the Employer or the Employer's Representative, provide such information to members of the Professional Team, the D&M Contractor, any purchaser or mortgagee referred to in clause 10.5 and any or all of the Tenants.

3.5 The Architect acknowledges that the requirements and objectives of the Employer set out in or inferred from the Brief are reasonable and attainable. The Architect shall perform all the services to be provided by him hereunder having due regard to the provisions of the Brief, but not so as to exclude the exercise of independent judgment on the part of the Architect. Nothing contained in the Brief shall relieve the Architect from any of his obligations or liabilities to the Employer under this Agreement.

3.6 The Employer intends to enter into a D&M Contract with the D&M Contractor in or substantially in the form of the draft D&M Contract previously made available to the Architect, and the Architect acknowledges that he has had a reasonable opportunity of inspecting the draft D&M Contract (other than the financial details or any other details which at the date hereof have not been agreed with the D&M Contractor).

3.7 In performing the services to be provided by him hereunder the Architect shall ensure that variations under Pre-Ordered Trade Contract Packages, the D&M Contract and trade contracts let or assumed by the D&M Contractor under the D&M Contract are not required in consequence of any negligence, default or breach of contract on the part of the Architect.

3.8 In performing the services to be provided by him hereunder the Architect shall comply with any Act of Parliament, any instrument, rule or order made under any Act of Parliament and any regulation or byelaw of any local authority or of any statutory undertaker or of any public or private utility or undertaking which has any jurisdiction with regard to the Works or the Site or with whose systems or property the Works or the Site are or will be connected.

3.9 In the event of any damage to or destruction of the Works or any part thereof the Architect shall provide such further services in connection with the reinstatement of the Works as the Employer may require, and all such further services provided by the Architect hereunder shall constitute Additional Services.

4. ADDITIONAL SERVICES

4.1 The Employer's Representative may require the Architect to carry out "Additional Services". Additional Services shall mean any services which are:-

4.1.1 not included in the Pre-Construction Services or the Construction Services, which arise by reason of a material change in the design of the Works and which would result in the Architect undertaking substantial extra work in relation thereto; or

4.1.2 performed by the Architect under this Agreement in relation to any Fitting-Out Works which the Employer, whether of its own volition or pursuant to any agreement or agreements for lease which it has entered into with Tenants, may agree to carry out (other than by way of a variation under the D&M Contract); or

4.1.3 referred to as Additional Services in clause 3.9 or 12.4.

For the avoidance of doubt, any services which the Architect is required to provide in consequence of any negligence, default or breach of contract on his part shall not constitute Additional Services and shall form part of the Services.

4.2 The Architect shall not commence any Additional Services without first being instructed to do so by the Employer's Representative. If the Architect considers that he is being required to carry out Additional Services he shall immediately give to the Employer and the Employer's Representative written notice thereof, together with a written statement of the fees for providing the Additional Services (if appropriate) and an estimate of the cost, time and programme implications (if any) to the Works of carrying out the same.

5. LIMITATIONS ON ARCHITECT'S AUTHORITY

Notwithstanding anything to the contrary contained in this Agreement, the Architect shall not (save in an emergency where there is a risk of damage to the Works or any other property or of death or personal injury) without the prior written consent of the Employer's Representative:-

5.1 make or approve any alteration to or from the work described in the Brief or the Employer's Requirements; or

5.2 make or approve or do anything which would or might increase the approved costs for the Works; or

5.3 make or approve or do anything which would or might affect the Pre-Contract Programme, the Construction Programme or the scheduled date from time to time for the completion of the Works.

6. BUDGET

6.1 In performing all the services to be provided by him hereunder, the Architect shall adhere to the Budget. No change to any cost estimate or allowance set out in the Budget shall be made until it has been sanctioned by the Employer's Representative.

6.2 If, without the prior written consent of the Employer's Representative, the cost of any work designed or to be carried out by the Architect or upon his recommendation is likely to exceed the relevant cost estimates or allowances contained in the Budget, the Employer may, without prejudice to any other rights or remedies it may possess, require the Architect at his own expense to re-design the relevant work.

7. ARCHITECT'S PERSONNEL

7.1 The Architect shall ensure that:-

7.1.1 the persons listed in Paragraph B of the First Schedule are engaged in the performance of all the services to be provided hereunder during the Pre-Construction Stage; and

7.1.2 the persons listed in Paragraph C of the First Schedule are engaged in the performance of all the services to be provided hereunder during the Construction Stage.

The Architect shall also provide at no further charge to the Employer such additional staff and assistance of suitable qualification and experience as may be necessary to ensure the proper performance by the Architect of all the services to be provided by him hereunder in accordance with this Agreement.

7.2 The personnel referred to in clause 7.1.2 shall not become involved in any way whatsoever with any of the services to be performed by the Architect under the D&M Contractor's Appointment and, without prejudice to the generality of clause 2.1, shall at all times act in the best interests of the Employer.

7.3 The Architect shall not remove or replace any of the persons referred to in clause 7.1 without the prior written approval of the Employer, which approval shall not be unreasonably withheld. Any replacement personnel must be approved by the Employer.

8. PATENT AND INTELLECTUAL PROPERTY RIGHTS

The Architect shall indemnify and save harmless the Employer from and against any and all losses, damages, claims, proceedings, costs and expenses suffered or incurred by the Employer by reason of the Architect infringing or being held to have infringed any patent or other intellectual property rights.

9. INSURANCES

9.1 Without prejudice to his obligations under this Agreement or otherwise at law, the Architect shall, subject to clause 9.2, maintain with well-established insurers or underwriters of repute to be approved by the Employer (such approval not to be unreasonably withheld) professional indemnity and public liability insurances to cover claims arising under this Agreement with limits of indemnity of not less than the levels of insurance cover required by the Employer and stated or referred to in Paragraph D of the First Schedule for any one occurrence or series of occurrences arising out of any one event.

9.2 The Architect shall maintain the insurances referred to in clause 9.1 for so long as any liability may arise under this Agreement, provided that such insurances are available in the market at commercially reasonable rates.

9.3 As and when he is reasonably required to do so by the Employer, the Architect shall produce for inspection a copy of the insurance policy or policies referred to in clause 9.1 or (if the disclosure of such policy or policies is expressly precluded by the terms thereof) a certificate or certificates of insurance in respect thereof and, in both cases, such other documentary evidence as may be necessary to show that the insurances required are being properly maintained.

9.4 If for any reason the Architect does not maintain the insurances required by clause 9.1 in accordance with clauses 9.1 and 9.2, or if the said insurances are maintained subject to conditions which would be of interest to a prudent client, or if he becomes aware of any circumstances which may render the said insurances void or otherwise unenforceable, the Architect shall notify the Employer immediately upon becoming aware thereof.

9.5 The Architect shall not without the prior written consent of the

Employer settle, waive or otherwise compromise any actual, anticipated or potential claim he may from time to time have against the insurers or underwriters of the insurance policies referred to in clause 9.1.

10. WARRANTIES

10.1 The Architect warrants to the Employer that in respect of all the services performed or to be performed by him in relation to the Works (whether under this Agreement or the D&M Contractor's Appointment) he has exercised and will continue to exercise all the skill, care and diligence to be reasonably expected of a properly qualified and competent architect who is experienced in carrying out such services for a development of a similar nature, size, scope, complexity and value to the Works.

10.2 Without prejudice to clause 10.1, the Architect warrants to the Employer that:-

10.2.1 the design for the Works, insofar as the same has been or will be prepared by the Architect or is otherwise the responsibility of the Architect, will satisfy the requirements set out in or reasonably to be inferred from the Brief;

10.2.2 he has not and will not select or approve for use or knowingly allow to be used in any part of the Works any materials or goods generally known at the time of use to be deleterious or otherwise not in accordance with good building practice or techniques; and

10.2.3 if instructed by the Employer to enter into the D&M Contractor's Appointment, he will promptly and efficiently comply with the terms thereof and fulfil his duties and obligations set out therein.

10.3 The Architect shall indemnify and save harmless the Employer from and against any and all losses, damages, expenses, liabilities, claims, costs or proceedings whatsoever arising from any breach by the Architect of this Agreement.

10.4 Nothing contained in this Agreement, no enquiry, inspection or advice which may be made or given by or on behalf of the Employer, the Employer's Representative, any member of the Professional Team, the D&M Contractor or any other person and no approval, comment, sanction, consent or decision at any time given to the Architect shall exclude or limit the Architect's liability for any breach of his duties and obligations under this Agreement.

10.5 The Architect shall upon the Employer's request forthwith execute a warranty agreement or agreements in the relevant form set out in the Fourth Schedule in favour of any bank or other funding institution providing finance for all or any part of the Works and/or in favour of any purchaser and/or mortgagee of the Site or the completed Works or any part thereof and/or in favour of any or all of the Tenants. The Architect shall before the execution thereof give a copy of the form of warranty agreement to his professional indemnity insurers or underwriters, and copies of the executed warranty agreements shall be given to such insurers or underwriters upon each renewal of his professional indemnity insurance.

11. ASSIGNMENT AND SUB-LETTING

11.1 The Architect shall not assign, novate, transfer or sub-let any right or obligation under this Agreement without the prior written consent of the Employer. No sub-letting or consent to sub-let shall in any way relieve the Architect from his responsibilities under this Agreement for the supply of all the services to be provided hereunder in accordance with the provisions herein contained or from any other of his responsibilities, obligations or liabilities.

11.2 The Employer may novate or assign this Agreement or the benefit hereof in whole or in part to any purchaser or mortgagee of the Site or the completed Works or any part thereof or to any of the Tenants or to any subsidiary or holding company of the Employer ("subsidiary" and "holding company" having for this purpose the meanings ascribed thereto by Section 736 of the Companies Act 1985), but the Employer shall not otherwise assign or novate this Agreement or the benefit hereof without the written consent of the Architect, which shall not be unreasonably withheld or delayed.

12. D&M CONTRACTOR'S APPOINTMENT

12.1 The Employer may instruct the Architect to enter into an agreement with the D&M Contractor for the provision of professional services during the Construction Stage, and the Architect shall immediately comply with any such instruction. Such agreement ("the D&M Contractor's Appointment") shall be in the form set out in the Sixth Schedule (subject to any amendments the Employer may reasonably require) and will be executed as a deed by the Architect and the D&M Contractor.

12.2 The Employer shall not be liable to the Architect for any loss of profit, loss of contracts or other losses and/or expenses arising out of or in connection with the Employer's failure for any reason to issue to the Architect an instruction pursuant to clause 12.1.

12.3 Notwithstanding his entry into the D&M Contractor's Appointment, the Architect shall continue to perform all of his duties and comply with all of his obligations arising under this Agreement insofar as the same remain to be performed or complied with.

12.4 If for any reason no instruction pursuant to clause 12.1 is issued to the Architect, or if the D&M Contractor's Appointment is terminated for any reason whatsoever, the Employer shall be entitled to require the Architect to carry out and complete some or all of the services which the Architect was to have carried out under the D&M Contractor's Appointment, and all such services provided by the Architect hereunder shall constitute Additional Services.

12.5 Upon any termination of the Architect's appointment under the D&M Contractor's Appointment the Architect shall deliver to the Employer all the Design Information and models prepared, used or provided by the Architect thereunder (whether in the course of preparation or completed).

13. COPYRIGHT AND CONFIDENTIALITY

13.1 Copyright in all drawings, designs, graphic materials and all computer programs, reports, specifications, calculations, visual aids and other information and documents which are or may be the subject of copyright and which have been or shall be prepared or used by or on behalf of the Architect in the course of performing all the services to be provided by him under this Agreement or the D&M Contractor's Appointment ("the Design Information") shall remain in the Architect.

13.2 The Architect as beneficial owner hereby grants to the Employer on a royalty-free, irrevocable and non-exclusive basis the full right and licence, for the full period during which copyright subsists in the Design Information, to use and reproduce the same and the designs contained therein (whether reprographically or otherwise, and whether by running or storing in memory any computer program or otherwise) for all purposes connected with the Works or the completed Works or any part thereof, including, without limitation, the design, construction, completion, use, operation, maintenance, extension, repair, reinstatement, advertisement, mortgaging, letting or sale thereof. Such licence shall carry the right to grant sub- licences and shall be transferable by the Employer to third parties.

13.3 Ownership and all intellectual property rights in models provided by the Architect (whether under this Agreement or the D&M Contractor's Appointment) and for which the Employer has paid the Architect shall vest in the Employer. Until such time as ownership and all intellectual property rights vest in it, the Employer shall have a licence on the terms described in clause 13.2 to use all models provided by the Architect.

13.4 Save as may reasonably be necessary in the proper performance of his duties under this Agreement, the Architect shall not at any time without the prior written consent of the Employer disclose to any person or otherwise make use of any of the Design Information, models, this Agreement or any of the documents or information referred to in this Agreement, any photographs of the Works or any confidential information relating to the Works or the Employer.

14. REMUNERATION

14.1 The remuneration payable to the Architect in respect of all the services to be provided under this Agreement (other than any Additional Services for which the Architect is entitled to receive additional payment) shall be the fees specified in the Third Schedule, which fees are inclusive of all expenses and disbursements (other than the reimbursable expenses and disbursements identified in the Third Schedule), overheads and profit, but exclusive of Value Added Tax. Payments to the Architect shall be made in accordance with the provisions of the Third Schedule.

14.2 If the Architect is instructed to provide Additional Services, then he shall be entitled to receive an additional payment therefor if the cost of the works or services to which they relate is not included in the Final Prime Cost. Where the Architect is entitled to any additional payment, the Employer may direct that the remuneration for the same is fixed at the amount specified in the Architect's written statement referred to in clause 4.2 or is calculated by reference to the time properly spent on the relevant Additional Services in accordance with any hourly rates for personnel which the Employer shall have previously agreed with the Architect. Any such fixed fee or hourly rates shall be inclusive of all expenses and disbursements (other than any reimbursable expenses and disbursements identified in the Third Schedule), overheads and profit, but exclusive of Value Added Tax, and shall be paid at a time and in instalments to be agreed by the Architect with the Employer.

14.3 The Architect shall not be entitled to receive payment for any further services provided pursuant to clause 3.9 where such damage or destruction was caused or contributed to by any act, omission, negligence, default or breach of contract on the part of the Architect.

15. EMPLOYER'S OBLIGATIONS AND EMPLOYER'S REPRESENTATIVE

15.1 The Employer shall supply and shall procure that the Employer's Representative shall supply to the Architect without charge, and as soon as is reasonably practicable after being requested so to do, all necessary and relevant data and information in their possession (including, without limitation, all relevant specifications and plant schedules). In addition, the Employer shall give and shall procure that the Employer's Representative shall give such assistance as shall reasonably be requested by the Architect to enable him to carry out and complete the services to be provided by him hereunder.

15.2 As soon as is reasonably practicable after being requested so to do, the Employer shall give and shall procure that the Employer's Representative shall give their comments, decisions and instructions on all sketches, drawings, reports, recommendations and other matters properly referred to either of them by the Architect.

15.3 Before the same are entered into or as soon as possible thereafter, the Employer shall supply the Architect with one copy of all contracts entered into by the Employer in respect of Pre- Ordered Trade Contract Packages. The Employer may omit from any such copies financial or other details which are of a confidential nature.

15.4 The Employer's Representative shall be the fully authorised representative of the Employer in respect of all matters arising hereunder and in connection with the Works. Save only as expressly provided in this Agreement, the Architect shall accept instructions from the Employer concerning the Works only from the Employer's Representative and shall communicate with the Employer through the Employer's Representative.

15.5 The Employer may at any time by written notice to the Architect appoint such other person as the Employer shall nominate to be its representative in place of the Employer's Representative and/or assume such of the rights or powers of the Employer's Representative under this Agreement as may be specified in such notice. The Employer's Representative for the time being shall act with the full authority of the Employer unless and until the Employer notifies the Architect of any change of representative or limitation of authority.

16. SUSPENSION OF SERVICES

16.1 The Employer may by written notice to the Architect require the

Architect to suspend performance of any or all of the services to be provided by the Architect hereunder. The Architect shall be entitled to be paid for the suspended services performed up to the date of suspension on the basis set out in clause 18.2.

16.2 The Employer may at any time by 14 Days' written notice require the Architect to resume the performance of the suspended services. In such event any payment made pursuant to clause 16.1 shall rank as a payment on account towards the payments to be made to the Architect under this Agreement.

17. TERMINATION OF ARCHITECT'S APPOINTMENT

17.1 If the Works are cancelled either the Employer or the Architect may by written notice to the other forthwith terminate the Architect's appointment.

17.2 If the Architect fails to carry out any of his duties in accordance with this Agreement or shall in any other way default in any of his obligations hereunder the Employer may give to the Architect written notice specifying the default. If such default shall thereafter continue for a further 14 Days the Employer may, without prejudice to any other rights or remedies, forthwith terminate the Architect's appointment by written notice to the Architect.

17.3 Without prejudice to clauses 17.1 and 17.2, the Employer may terminate the Architect's appointment hereunder at any time by giving 14 Days' written notice.

18. CONSEQUENCES OF TERMINATION OF ARCHITECT'S APPOINTMENT

18.1 Upon any termination of the Architect's appointment the Architect shall deliver to the Employer all the Design Information and any models prepared, used or provided by the Architect (whether in the course of preparation or completed).

18.2 If the Architect's appointment is terminated under clause 17.1 or 17.3 the Employer shall pay to the Architect a fair and reasonable proportion of the remuneration payable to the Architect under this Agreement, such proportion to be commensurate with the services properly performed by the Architect in accordance with this Agreement up to the date of such termination less any amounts previously paid by the Employer to the Architect. The Employer shall also pay to the Architect the net cost of any reimbursable expenses and disbursements referred to in the Third Schedule which have been properly incurred by the Architect prior to such termination.

18.3 If the Architect's appointment is terminated under clause 17.2 the Employer shall be entitled, without prejudice to any other rights or remedies, to set off any sums accrued due but unpaid at the date of such termination against any loss or damage it may sustain as a result of such termination (including, without limitation, the cost of engaging others to carry out and complete the services which were to have been provided hereunder) or of any antecedent breach of the Architect's obligations hereunder, and save for any balance then remaining payable no further payment shall be made to the Architect.

18.4 The Employer shall not be liable to the Architect for any loss of profit, loss of contracts or other losses and/or expenses arising out of or in connection with any termination of the Architect's appointment or of this Agreement.

18.5 Termination of the Architect's appointment shall, subject to clause 18.4, be without prejudice to the rights and remedies of either party in relation to any negligence, default or breach of contract of the other prior to such termination.

19. SETTLEMENT OF DISPUTES

19.1 The "Adjudicator" for the purposes of this Agreement shall mean the person named as such in Paragraph E of the First Schedule or such other person as may be appointed from time to time under clause 19.4 to act as Adjudicator in place of the Adjudicator so named.

19.2 If any dispute or difference of any kind whatsoever shall arise between the Employer (and/or the Employer's Representative) on the one hand and the Architect on the other hand at any time prior to the completion or alleged completion of all the services to be provided hereunder or the termination or alleged termination of the Architect's appointment hereunder, then such dispute or difference shall in the first place be referred to and settled by the Adjudicator who, within a period of 7 Days after being requested by either party to do so, shall give written notice of his decision to the Employer and the Architect. Each such dispute or difference shall be the subject of a separate reference. No such reference shall relieve either party from any liability for the due and punctual performance of its obligations under this Agreement. The Adjudicator's decision on any matter referred to him under this clause shall be confined (and each such reference shall be expressly so limited in its terms) to a decision in favour of the position taken in the reference by one or other of the parties in the matter, and the Adjudicator accordingly shall not be empowered to effect in his decision at that stage a compromise between the two such positions unless both parties shall otherwise agree. The Adjudicator shall determine which party shall bear the cost of any reference to him, or in which proportions the parties shall bear such costs, and such costs shall be paid within 30 Days of the date of his decision.

19.3 In giving a decision under clause 19.2 the Adjudicator shall be deemed to be acting as expert and not as arbitrator, and his decision under clause 19.2 shall be final and binding upon the parties until the completion or alleged completion of all the services to be provided hereunder or the termination or alleged termination of the Architect's appointment hereunder and shall forthwith be given effect to by the Architect, who shall proceed with all the services to be provided hereunder with all due diligence whether or not either party gives notice to the other of its intention to refer the matter to the High Court as provided in clause 19.5. The exercise of the Adjudicator's powers shall also be subject to any other terms agreed between the parties and with him and incorporated into the document appointing him to act (which shall be based upon the form set out in the Seventh Schedule and which shall be signed by both parties).

19.4 If the Adjudicator fails to give his decision in accordance with the provisions of clause 19.2 or if he shall be unable or refuse to act, then all disputes or differences under clause 19.2 shall be referred to and settled by a substitute Adjudicator to be agreed between the parties or, failing agreement within 7 Days after either party has given to the other a written request to concur in the appointment of a substitute Adjudicator, a person to be appointed upon the application of either party by the Chairman for the time being of the Chartered Institute of Arbitrators to act as substitute Adjudicator for all the purposes of this Agreement.

19.5 If the substitute Adjudicator appointed under clause 19.4 refuses or neglects to give a decision or if, upon receipt of the Adjudicator's notice of his decision under clause 19.2 or the substitute Adjudicator's decision under clause 19.4, either party is dissatisfied with the same, then either party may, within 30 Days after such refusal or after receiving the Adjudicator's or substitute Adjudicator's notice of his decision, give notice to the other of its intention to refer the matter to the High Court of Justice in London for determination in accordance with clause 19.6. If no such notice is given by either party within 30 Days from receipt of notice of the Adjudicator's or substitute Adjudicator's decision such decision shall remain final and binding upon the parties.

19.6 All disputes or differences under clause 19.2 in respect of which a decision (if any) of the Adjudicator or substitute Adjudicator has not become final and binding under clause 19.5, and all other disputes or differences arising out of or in connection with this Agreement or any of the services to be provided hereunder as to any matter or thing of whatsoever nature, shall, unless the parties agree to the contrary, be referred for decision to the High Court of Justice in London to be tried by a Judge sitting as such and not as an arbitrator. Such reference shall not be made until after completion or alleged completion of all the services to be provided hereunder or the termination or alleged termination of the Architect's appointment hereunder, except with the written consent of the Employer and the Architect.

19.7 The Judge who tries any dispute or difference referred for decision to the High Court in accordance with clause 19.6 shall, without prejudice to the generality of his powers, have full power to open up, review and revise any decision, opinion, direction, certificate or valuation of the Employer and/or the Employer's Representative (except in respect of any matter or thing expressly left by the terms of this Agreement to its or his discretion) or of the Adjudicator or substitute Adjudicator and to direct such measurements and/or valuations as may in his opinion be desirable in order to determine the rights of the parties.

20. GOVERNING LAW

This Agreement shall be governed by and interpreted in accordance with English law, and the Employer and the Architect hereby submit to the jurisdiction of the English Courts.

21. MISCELLANEOUS

21.1 Words importing the singular only shall also include the plural and vice versa, and where the context requires words importing persons shall include firms and corporations.

21.2 This Agreement supersedes any previous agreements or arrangements between the parties in respect of the services to be provided hereunder and represents the entire understanding between the parties in relation thereto.

21.3 Any notice to be served under this Agreement shall be served personally, by facsimile transmission, by telex or by first class pre-paid post. The addresses for service of the Employer and the Architect shall be those stated in this Agreement or such other address as the party to be served may have previously notified in writing. Any notice, if delivered personally, shall be deemed to have been served at the time of delivery or, if sent by facsimile transmission or by telex, shall be deemed to have been served at the time of transmission (but shall nevertheless be confirmed by first class pre-paid post) or, if sent by post, shall be deemed to have been served on the second business day following posting.

EITHER
[21.4 The term "Architect" includes any additional partners who may be admitted into the partnership of the Architect during the currency of this Agreement. This Agreement shall not automatically terminate upon the death, retirement or resignation of any partner in the Architect, and the rights, obligations and liabilities of the partners in the Architect are joint and several.]

OR
[21.4 The Architect shall deliver to the Employer upon the execution of this Agreement a guarantee of his obligations and liabilities hereunder duly executed under seal by [the Architect's ultimate holding company/the directors for the time being of the Architect] in the form set out in the [Ninth] Schedule, and the Employer shall not be liable to make any payment under this Agreement until the Architect has complied with this clause.]

IN WITNESS whereof the Employer and [all the partners in] the Architect have executed this Agreement as a deed on the date first before written.

FIRST SCHEDULE
A. The Employer's Representative is:-
. . . .

The members of the Professional Team are:-
. . . .

B. The Architect's personnel for the Pre-Construction Stage (see clause 7.1.1) are:-
. . . .

C. The Architect's personnel for the Construction Stage (see clause 7.1.2) are:-
. . . .

D. Details of minimum required professional indemnity cover (see clause 9.1):-

☐ Policy number: . . . .

☐ Expiry date: ....
☐ Limit of indemnity: ....
☐ Policy excess: ....
☐ Underwriters: ....
☐ Brokers: ....
☐ Minimum requirements of the Employer (which may be reviewed by the Employer):

....

Details of minimum required public liability cover (see clause 9.1):-

☐ Policy number: ....
☐ Expiry date: ....
☐ Limit of indemnity: ....
☐ Policy excess: ....
☐ Underwriters: ....
☐ Brokers: ....
☐ Minimum requirements of the Employer (which may be reviewed by the Employer):

....

E. The Adjudicator referred to in clause 19.1 is:-

....

SECOND SCHEDULE: SCOPE OF SERVICES

PART A – PRE-CONSTRUCTION SERVICES
The Pre-Construction Services, which are to be performed by the Architect during the Pre-Construction Stage and thereafter as necessary, are:-

[To be inserted]

PART B – CONSTRUCTION SERVICES
The Construction Services, which are to be performed by the Architect during the Construction Stage, are:-

[To be inserted]

THIRD SCHEDULE: REMUNERATION AND TERMS OF PAYMENT
1. The total fee payable to the Architect for all services to be provided under both this Agreement and the D&M Contractor's Appointment (other than the preparation of the Employer's Requirements and any Additional Services) shall be [..................] per cent of the Final Prime Cost after deducting any payments made to sub-consultants under the sub-consultancy agreements. The proportion of such total fee payable under this Agreement shall be such proportion thereof as is equivalent to the proportion of such services which are provided by the Architect to the Employer up the date on which the Architect shall enter into the D&M Contractor's Appointment. The fee payable for the preparation of the Employer's Requirements shall be [..................] per cent of the Anticipated Target Cost. The fee payable for any Additional Services shall be as described in clause 14.2.

2. [Terms of payment to be agreed and inserted.]

3. The reimbursable expenses and disbursements will be the net costs properly incurred by the Architect, as substantiated by invoices, vouchers and other documents to the reasonable satisfaction of the Employer's Representative, in respect of the following expenses and disbursements (if previously authorised or requested in writing by the Employer's Representative):-

3.1 reasonable hotel bills;

3.2 international travel and reasonable subsistence costs overseas;

3.3 models; and

3.4 printing costs for reports and tender documentation.

FOURTH SCHEDULE: FORMS OF WARRANTY AGREEMENT
REFERRED TO IN CLAUSE 10.5
[To be inserted]

FIFTH SCHEDULE

PART A – BRIEF
[To be inserted]

PART B – EMPLOYER'S REQUIREMENTS
[To be inserted]

SIXTH SCHEDULE: FORM OF D&M CONTRACTOR'S
APPOINTMENT REFERRED TO IN CLAUSE 12.1
Dated ....

[D&M Contractor] and [Architect]

Architect's sub-consultancy agreement relating to ....

ARCHITECT'S SUB-CONSULTANCY AGREEMENT

CONTENTS
Clauses

THIS AGREEMENT is made on ....

BETWEEN
1. [.................................] whose registered office is at
[....] ("the D&M Contractor"),
and

2. The partners in [..............................] being the persons
listed in the [Fifth] Schedule of/[.................................]
LIMITED whose registered office is at [.............................]
("the Architect").

RECITALS
(A) – [.................................] whose registered office is at
[....] ("the Employer") intends
to proceed with [the demolition of the existing building,] the design and
construction of [....]
and, if the Employer so elects, the design and construction of the
Landlord's Works (as defined in the D&M Contract) at [..............
.................................] ("the Project").

(B) – By an agreement dated [....................................]
("the D&M Contract") the Employer has engaged the D&M Contractor to
provide advice and assistance in the planning, organisation and
programming of the Project and to advise on the outline design for the
Project during the Pre-Construction Stage (as defined in the D&M Contract)
and, if instructed by the Employer, to complete or procure the completion
of the detailed design for the Project and to procure, manage, organise and
continually supervise the construction of the Project during the
Construction Stage (as defined in the D&M Contract).

(C) – The Architect has entered into an agreement dated [.............]
("the Appointment") with the Employer for the supply of professional services
as more particularly described therein during both the Pre-Construction Stage
and the Construction Stage (as defined in the D&M Contract).

(D) – The Project is at the date hereof in the Construction Stage (as defined in D&M Contract), the Employer having opted under the D&M Contract to proceed with the D&M Contractor, and the D&M Contract includes the documents agreed between the Employer and the D&M Contractor and inserted in Appendix B of the D&M Contract.

(E) – Pursuant to the provisions of the D&M Contract and the Appointment, the D&M Contractor and the Architect have agreed to enter into this Agreement for the provision of the Services and the Additional Services, if any, on the terms and conditions herein contained.

(F) – The D&M Contractor and, subject to clause 11.3, the Employer have relied and will continue to rely upon the Architect's skill and judgment in respect of all matters covered by this Agreement.

NOW IT IS HEREBY AGREED as follows:-

1. DEFINITIONS

1.1 In this Agreement expressions defined in the D&M Contract have the meanings respectively therein given (unless a contrary meaning is indicated in any of the provisions of this Agreement), expressions defined in the Recitals hereto shall have the meanings therein given, and the following expressions shall have the following meanings:-

"Additional Services" – see clause 5.1;

"Appointment" – see Recital C;

"D&M Contract" – see Recital B (a copy of the D&M Contract, other than the financial details, is set out in the Fourth Schedule);

"Design Information" – see clause 14.1;

"Employer" – see Recital A;

"Project" – See Recital A;

"Services" means the services referred to in clause 4.1 and in the Second Schedule.

1.2 References in this Agreement to statutory or regulatory provisions shall be construed as references to those provisions as respectively amended or re-enacted from time to time (whether before or after the date of this Agreement) and shall include any provisions of which they are re-enactments (with or without modification) and any subordinate legislation made under such provisions.

2. APPOINTMENT

2.1 The D&M Contractor hereby appoints the Architect, and the Architect hereby agrees to carry out and complete the Services and the Additional Services, if any, fully and faithfully and upon the terms and conditions set out in this Agreement.

2.2 The appointment of the Architect shall be deemed to have commenced with effect from the date upon which the Architect shall have begun to perform the services to be performed hereunder.

3. APPLICATION OF D&M CONTRACT

3.1 The Architect undertakes with the D&M Contractor that he will:-

3.1.1 observe, perform and comply with all the provisions of the D&M Contract on the part of the D&M Contractor to be observed, performed and complied with during the Construction Stage, insofar as they relate and apply to this Agreement and are not inconsistent with its express provisions; and

3.1.2 perform all the services to be provided hereunder so that no act or omission on the part of the Architect or any of his employees, agents or sub-contractors shall constitute, cause or contribute to any breach by the D&M Contractor of any of its obligations under the D&M Contract, and the Architect shall, save where the provisions of this Agreement otherwise expressly require, assume and perform under this Agreement all the obligations assumed and to be performed by the D&M Contractor under the D&M Contract insofar as they relate to any and all of the services to be provided hereunder.

3.2 The Architect acknowledges that any breach by him of this Agreement may result in the D&M Contractor committing a breach of and becoming liable in damages or otherwise under the D&M Contract and any other contract to which the D&M Contractor is a party in connection with the Project and agrees that any and all such liability is within his reasonable contemplation at the time of entering into this Agreement as being a likely consequence of any breach by him of the terms of this Agreement. The Architect shall be fully liable to the D&M Contractor for any breach of the terms of this Agreement, including, without limitation, for any liability of whatsoever nature which the D&M Contractor may incur to the Employer under or for breach of the D&M Contract by reason of the negligence, default or breach of contract of the Architect or his employees, agents or sub-contractors.

3.3 Without prejudice to clause 3.2, the Architect, having notice of the terms of the D&M Contract, undertakes not to contend, whether in any legal action or proceedings or otherwise, that the D&M Contractor has suffered or incurred no damage, loss or expense or that the Architect's liability to the D&M Contractor should be in any way reduced or extinguished by reason of clause 14 of the D&M Contract.

4. ARCHITECT'S OBLIGATIONS

4.1 As part of the Services, the Architect shall:-

4.1.1 carry out and complete the development of the design for the Project which has been prepared by him under the Appointment in accordance with the Employer's Requirements;

4.1.2 examine the designs prepared or to be prepared by the Sub-Consultants for compliance with the designs prepared or to be prepared by the Architect and, insofar as they relate to or affect the Architect's designs, with the Employer's Requirements and the instructions and reasonable requirements of the D&M Contractor, and co-ordinate and integrate all such designs into the overall design for the Project;

4.1.3 examine the design development work and detailed designs prepared or to be prepared by Trade Contractors for compliance with the designs prepared or to be prepared by the Architect and, insofar as they relate to or affect the Architect's designs, with the Employer's Requirements and the instructions and reasonable requirements of the D&M Contractor, and co-ordinate and integrate all such design development work and detailed designs into the overall design for the Project;

4.1.4 provide all advice, drawings, information, documents, consents, comments, approvals, details, specifications, instructions and directions required from the Architect in connection with the Project promptly, efficiently and in good time so as not to delay or disrupt the progress of the Project;

4.1.5 upon request or otherwise in accordance with any schedules for the release of the same which may be agreed with the D&M Contractor, provide the D&M Contractor, Sub-Consultants and Trade Contractors without charge with such copies of all drawings, details, specifications, reports and other information in respect of the Project which have been prepared or used by the Architect as they may reasonably require; and

4.1.6 without charge provide the D&M Contractor with such details, vouchers and supporting documentation contemplated by clause 29.1 of the D&M Contract for the purposes of adjusting the Target Cost or the Adjusted Target Cost as the D&M Contractor may request.

4.2 The Architect shall forthwith comply with all instructions and directions issued to him in writing by the D&M Contractor, save that where the Architect makes reasonable objection thereto in writing to the D&M Contractor within seven Days of receipt thereof such instruction or direction shall not take effect unless confirmed in writing by the D&M Contractor. If, within seven Days after receipt of any instruction, direction or written confirmation thereof from the D&M Contractor, the Architect does not comply therewith, then the D&M Contractor may, without prejudice to any other rights or remedies it may possess in relation thereto, employ and pay others to execute any work which may be necessary to give effect to such instruction or direction and deduct all costs incurred in connection with such employment from any sums payable to the Architect under this Agreement.

4.3 The Architect shall provide all such services as the D&M Contractor may require in relation to any variation or proposed variation under the D&M Contract (including, without limitation, services required in respect of the Landlord's Works).

4.4 The Architect shall, in relation to any proposed variation under the D&M Contract, as soon as practicable provide the D&M Contractor with such specifications and estimates contemplated by clause 17.3 of the D&M Contract as the D&M Contractor shall request from the Architect. If the proposed variation under the D&M Contract is withdrawn by the Employer's Representative the Architect shall have no claim of any description in relation thereto.

4.5 The Architect shall proceed regularly and diligently with all the services to be provided by him hereunder in accordance with the time requirements set out in the Construction Programme and any schedules for the release of information which may be agreed with the D&M Contractor and without delaying and disrupting the services or works to be carried out by Sub-Consultants and Trade Contractors in consequence of any negligence, default or breach of contract on the part of the Architect. The Architect shall constantly use his best endeavours to prevent any delay or disruption to the progress of the Project and shall increase resources as necessary at his own expense in order to minimise any delays which become apparent.

4.6 The Architect shall at all times keep the D&M Contractor fully informed and shall provide it with regular reports on all matters of interest to a prudent design and management contractor, together with all such other information in regard to the Project as the D&M Contractor may require. In addition, the Architect shall, as and when requested to do so by the D&M Contractor, provide such information to the Sub-Consultants and Trade Contractors.

4.7 In performing the services to be provided by him hereunder the Architect shall comply with any Act of Parliament, any instrument, rule or order made under any Act of Parliament and any regulation or byelaw of any local authority or of any statutory undertaker or of any public or private utility or undertaking which has any jurisdiction with regard to the Project or the Site or with whose systems or property the Project or the Site are or will be connected.

4.8 In the event of any damage to or destruction of the Project or any part thereof the Architect shall provide such further services in connection with the reinstatement of the Project as the D&M Contractor may require, and all such further services provided by the Architect hereunder shall constitute Additional Services.

4.9 In performing the services to be provided by him hereunder the Architect shall ensure that variations under the D&M Contract are not required because of any negligence, default or breach of contract on the part of the Architect.

5. ADDITIONAL SERVICES

5.1 The D&M Contractor may require the Architect to carry out "Additional Services". Additional Services shall mean any services which are not included in the Services, which arise by reason of a material change in the design of the Project and which would result in the Architect undertaking substantial extra work in relation to the Project, or which are referred to as such in clause 4.8. For the avoidance of doubt, any services which the Architect is required to provide in consequence of any negligence, default or breach of contract on his part shall not constitute Additional Services and shall form part of the Services.

5.2 The Architect shall not commence any Additional Services without first being instructed to do so by the D&M Contractor. If the Architect considers that he is being required to carry out Additional Services he shall immediately give to the D&M Contractor written notice thereof, together with a written statement of the fees for providing the Additional Services (if appropriate) and an estimate of the cost, time and programme implications (if any) to the Project of carrying out the same.

6. LIMITATIONS ON ARCHITECT'S AUTHORITY

Notwithstanding anything to the contrary contained in this Agreement, the Architect shall not (save in an emergency where there is a risk of damage to the Project or any other property or of death or personal injury) without the prior written consent of the D&M Contractor:-

6.1 make or approve any alteration to or from the work described in the Employer's Requirements and any designs, details and specifications issued to Trade Contractors; or

6.2 make or approve or do anything which would or might increase the approved costs for the Project; or

6.3 make or approve or do anything which would or might affect the Construction Programme or the scheduled date from time to time for the completion of the Project.

7. BUDGET

7.1 In performing all the services to be provided by him hereunder, the Architect shall adhere to the Budget. No change to any cost estimate or allowance set out in the Budget shall be made until it has been sanctioned by the D&M Contractor and the Employer's Representative.

7.2 If the cost of any work designed or to be carried out by the Architect or upon his recommendation is likely to exceed the relevant cost estimates or allowances contained in the Budget, the D&M Contractor, without prejudice to any other rights or remedies it may possess, may require the Architect at his own expense to re-design the relevant work.

8. ARCHITECT'S PERSONNEL

8.1 The Architect shall ensure that the persons listed in Paragraph A of the First Schedule are engaged in the performance of all the services to be performed under this Agreement. The Architect shall also provide at no further charge to the D&M Contractor such additional staff and assistance of suitable qualification and experience as may be necessary to ensure the proper performance by the Architect of all the services to be provided by him hereunder in accordance with this Agreement.

8.2 The Architect shall not remove or replace any of the persons referred to in clause 8.1 without the prior written approval of the D&M Contractor, which approval shall not be unreasonably withheld. Any replacement personnel must be approved by the D&M Contractor.

9. PATENT AND INTELLECTUAL PROPERTY RIGHTS

The Architect shall indemnify and save harmless the Employer and the D&M Contractor from and against any and all losses, damages, claims, proceedings, costs and expenses suffered or incurred by the Employer and/or the D&M Contractor or to which either of them may be put by reason of the Architect infringing or being held to have infringed any patent or other intellectual property rights.

10. INSURANCES

10.1 Without prejudice to his obligations under this Agreement or otherwise at law, the Architect shall, subject to clause 10.2, maintain with well-established insurers or underwriters of repute to be approved by the D&M Contractor (such approval not to be unreasonably withheld) professional indemnity and public liability insurances to cover claims arising under this Agreement with limits of indemnity of not less than the levels of insurance cover required by the D&M Contractor and stated or referred to in Paragraph B of the First Schedule for any one occurrence or series of occurrences arising out of any one event.

10.2 The Architect shall maintain the insurances referred to in clause 10.1 for so long as any liability may arise under this Agreement, provided that such insurances are available in the market at commercially reasonable rates.

10.3 As and when it is reasonably required to do so by the D&M Contractor, the Architect shall produce for inspection a copy of the insurance policy or policies referred to in clause 10.1 or (if the disclosure of such policy or policies is expressly precluded by the terms thereof) a certificate or certificates of insurance in respect thereof and, in both cases, such other documentary evidence as may be necessary to show that the insurances required are being properly maintained.

10.4 If for any reason the Architect does not maintain the insurances required by clause 10.1 in accordance with clauses 10.1 and 10.2, or if the said insurances are maintained subject to conditions which would be of interest to a prudent client, or if he becomes aware of any circumstances which may render the said insurances void or otherwise unenforceable, the Architect shall notify the D&M Contractor immediately upon becoming aware thereof.

10.5 The Architect shall not without the prior written consent of the D&M Contractor settle, waive or otherwise compromise any actual, anticipated or potential claim he may from time to time have against the insurers or underwriters of the insurance policies referred to in clause 10.1.

11. WARRANTIES

11.1 The Architect warrants to the D&M Contractor that in respect of all the services to be provided by him under this Agreement he has exercised and will continue to exercise all the skill, care and diligence to be reasonably expected of a properly qualified and competent architect who is experienced in carrying out such services for a development of a similar nature, size, scope, complexity and value to the Project.

11.2 Without prejudice to clause 11.1, the Architect warrants to the D&M Contractor that he has not and will not select or approve for use or knowingly allow to be used in any part of the Project any materials or goods generally known at the time of their use to be deleterious or otherwise not in accordance with good building practice or techniques.

11.3 The Architect acknowledges that, in relation to any design to be carried out by the Architect or which is otherwise the responsibility of the Architect under this Agreement, the Employer will be relying on the skill and judgment of the Architect (as provided in clause 11.4 of the D&M Contract).

11.4 For the avoidance of doubt, the Architect agrees that no provision of this Agreement or the D&M Contract under which the consent or approval of the D&M Contractor, the Employer or any other person is required, no granting of any consent or approval and no enquiry, inspection or advice which may be made or given by or on behalf of the D&M Contractor, the Employer or any other person shall relieve the Architect of any liability or obligation under this Agreement for the carrying-out of the services to be provided hereunder in accordance with the provisions herein contained.

12. ASSIGNMENT AND SUB-LETTING

12.1 The Architect shall not without the prior written consent of the D&M Contractor assign this Agreement or sub-let the whole or any portion of the Services or any Additional Services. It shall be a condition of any such sub-letting that, subject to clause 18.3.2, the employment of any sub-contractor shall terminate upon the termination (for any reason) of the Architect's appointment hereunder.

12.2 No sub-letting or consent to sub-let shall in any way relieve the Architect from his responsibilities under this Agreement for the supply of all the services to be provided hereunder in accordance with the provisions herein contained or from any other of his responsibilities, obligations or liabilities under this Agreement.

13. APPOINTMENT BY EMPLOYER

Notwithstanding his entry into this Agreement, the Architect shall continue to perform all of his duties and comply with all of his obligations arising under the Appointment.

14. COPYRIGHT AND CONFIDENTIALITY

14.1 Copyright in all drawings, designs, graphic materials and all computer programs, reports, specifications, calculations, visual aids and other information and documents which are or may be the subject of copyright and which have been or shall be prepared or used by or on behalf of the Architect in the course of performing all the services to be provided by him hereunder ("the Design Information") shall remain in the Architect.

14.2 The Architect as beneficial owner hereby grants to the D&M Contractor on a royalty-free, irrevocable and non-exclusive basis the full right and licence, for the full period during which copyright subsists in the Design Information, to use and reproduce the same and the designs contained therein (whether reprographically or otherwise, and whether by running or storing in memory any computer program or otherwise) for all purposes connected with the Project or any part thereof, including, without limitation, the design, construction, completion, use, operation, maintenance, extension, repair, reinstatement, advertisement, mortgaging, letting or sale thereof. Such licence shall carry the right to grant sub-licences to Sub-Consultants and Trade Contractors for the performance of their respective duties and obligations in connection with the Project.

14.3 Save as may reasonably be necessary in the proper performance of his duties under this Agreement, the Architect shall not at any time without the prior written consent of the D&M Contractor disclose to any person or otherwise make use of any of the Design Information, this Agreement or any of the documents or information referred to in this Agreement, any photographs of the Project or any confidential information relating to the Project, the D&M Contractor or the Employer.

15. REMUNERATION

15.1 The remuneration payable to the Architect in respect of all the services to be provided under this Agreement (other than any Additional Services for which the Architect is entitled to receive additional payment) shall be the fees specified in the Third Schedule, which fees are inclusive of all expenses and disbursements (other than the reimbursable expenses and disbursements identified in the Third Schedule), overheads and profit, but exclusive of Value Added Tax. Payments to the Architect shall be made in accordance with the provisions of the Third Schedule.

15.2 If the Architect is instructed to provide Additional Services, then he shall be entitled to receive an additional payment therefor if the cost of the works or services to which they relate is not included in the Final Prime Cost. Where the Architect is entitled to any additional payment, the D&M Contractor may direct that the remuneration for the same is fixed at the amount specified in the Architect's written statement referred to in clause 5.2 or is calculated by reference to the time properly spent on the relevant Additional Services in accordance with any hourly rates for personnel which the D&M Contractor shall have previously agreed with the Architect. Any such fixed fee or hourly rates shall be inclusive of all expenses and disbursements (other than any reimbursable expenses and disbursements identified in the Third Schedule), overheads and profit, but exclusive of Value Added Tax, and shall be paid at a time and in instalments to be agreed by the Architect with the D&M Contractor.

15.3 The Architect shall not be entitled to receive payment for any further services provided pursuant to clause 4.8 where such damage or destruction was caused or contributed to by any act, omission, negligence, default or breach of contract on the part of the Architect.

16. D&M CONTRACTOR'S OBLIGATIONS

16.1 The D&M Contractor shall supply and shall procure that the Sub-Consultants and Trade Contractors shall supply to the Architect without charge and in accordance with the Construction Programme or as soon as is reasonably practicable after being requested so to do, all necessary and relevant data and information in their possession (including, without limitation, all relevant specifications and plant schedules). In addition, the D&M Contractor shall give and shall procure that the Sub-Consultants and Trade Contractors shall give such assistance as shall reasonably be requested by the Architect to enable him to carry out and complete the services to be provided by him hereunder.

16.2 As soon as is reasonably practicable after being requested so to do so as not to delay or disrupt the carrying-out of the services to be provided hereunder, the D&M Contractor shall give and shall procure that the Sub-Consultants and Trade Contractors shall give their comments, decisions and instructions on all sketches, drawings, reports, recommendations and other matters properly referred to them by the Architect.

17. TERMINATION OF ARCHITECT'S APPOINTMENT

17.1 If the Project is cancelled either the D&M Contractor or the Architect may by written notice to the other forthwith terminate the Architect's appointment.

17.2 If the Architect fails to carry out any of his duties in accordance with this Agreement or shall in any other way default in any of his obligations hereunder the D&M Contractor may give to the Architect written notice specifying the default. If such default shall thereafter continue for a further 14 Days the D&M Contractor may, without prejudice to any other rights or remedies, forthwith terminate the Architect's appointment by written notice to the Architect, provided that such notice shall not be given unreasonably or vexatiously.

17.3 The D&M Contractor shall, upon instruction from the Employer's Representative following the termination of the Appointment due to default on the part of the Architect, forthwith terminate the Architect's appointment hereunder by written notice to the Architect.

17.4 If the D&M Contractor shall fail to make any payment properly due to the Architect under this Agreement within 28 Days of the Architect's written notice to the D&M Contractor under this Agreement requiring such payment to be made, or if the D&M Contractor persistently fails to comply with its obligations hereunder in some other material way, the Architect may, without prejudice to any other rights or remedies, give to the D&M Contractor (with a copy to the Employer's Representative) written notice specifying the default and, if such default shall thereafter continue for a further 28 Days, the Architect may forthwith terminate his appointment by written notice to the D&M Contractor, provided that such notice shall not be given unreasonably or vexatiously.

17.5 If for any reason the D&M Contractor's employment under the D&M Contract is determined (whether by the D&M Contractor or by the Employer, and whether due to any default of the D&M Contractor or otherwise), then either:-

17.5.1 the Employer shall be entitled by written notice to the Architect in the name of the D&M Contractor to terminate forthwith the Architect's appointment hereunder; or

17.5.2 the D&M Contractor shall upon the Employer's request be entitled to assign or novate this Agreement to the Employer upon the terms specified in clause 26.5 of the D&M Contract, provided that no person subsequently appointed to perform the functions of the D&M Contractor (including the Employer) shall be entitled to disregard or overrule any previous certificate, decision or instruction given by the D&M Contractor for the time being.

18. CONSEQUENCES OF TERMINATION OF ARCHITECT'S APPOINTMENT

18.1 Upon any termination of the Architect's appointment the Architect shall deliver to the D&M Contractor all the Design Information (whether in the course of preparation or completed).

18.2 If the Architect's appointment is terminated under clauses 17.1, 17.4 or 17.5.1 the D&M Contractor shall pay to the Architect a fair and reasonable proportion of the remuneration payable to the Architect under this Agreement, such proportion to be commensurate with the services properly performed by the Architect in accordance with this Agreement up to the date of such termination less any amounts previously paid by the D&M Contractor to the Architect. The D&M Contractor shall also pay to the Architect the net cost of any reimbursable expenses and disbursements referred to in the Third Schedule which have been properly incurred by the Architect prior to such termination.

18.3 If the Architect's appointment is terminated under clauses 17.2 or 17.3:-

18.3.1 the D&M Contractor shall be entitled, without prejudice to any other rights or remedies, to set off any sums accrued due but unpaid at the date of such termination against any loss or damage it may sustain as a result of such termination (including, without limitation, the cost of engaging others to carry out and complete the services which were to have been provided hereunder) or of any antecedent breach of the Architect's obligations hereunder, and save for any balance then remaining payable no further payment shall be made to the Architect; and

18.3.2 the Architect shall upon the D&M Contractor's request assign to it the benefit of any agreement for the supply of services in connection with this Agreement, and the D&M Contractor may in such circumstances pay the supplier for any such performed services insofar as the price thereof has not already been paid by the Architect, and the D&M Contractor may deduct any such payments from any sums payable to the Architect under this Agreement or recover the same as a debt from the Architect.

18.4 The D&M Contractor shall not be liable to the Architect for any loss of profit, loss of contracts or other losses and/or expenses arising out of or in connection with any termination of the Architect's appointment or of this Agreement.

18.5 Termination of the Architect's appointment shall, subject to clause 18.4, be without prejudice to the rights and remedies of either party in relation to any negligence, default or breach of contract of the other prior to such termination.

19. SETTLEMENT OF DISPUTES

19.1 The provisions of clause 36 of the D&M Contract shall apply to this Agreement as between the D&M Contractor and the Architect for the settling of any dispute or difference that may arise between them as if such provisions were here set out in full, but:-

19.1.1 as if references therein to the Employer and/or the Employer's

Representative and to the D&M Contractor were references to the D&M Contractor and to the Architect respectively;

19.1.2 excluding all references therein to Prime Cost and to the Target Cost;

19.1.3 as if in line 3 of clause 36.2 the words "the issue of the certificate" to the end of clause 36.2.5 (inclusive) were replaced by "the completion or alleged completion of all the services to be provided hereunder or the termination or alleged termination of the Architect's appointment hereunder", and as if the words "and in particular" to "any other such clauses" (inclusive) in lines 27 to 32 were deleted;

19.1.4 as if references to the design and construction of the Works were references to the services to be performed under this Agreement;

19.1.5 as if references to Practical Completion of the Final Section of Works were references to the completion or alleged completion of all the services to be provided under this Agreement; and

19.1.6 otherwise mutatis mutandis (for example, as regards clause cross-references).

19.2 The Adjudicator for the purposes of this Agreement shall be the person so named or appointed under the D&M Contract. The exercise of the Adjudicator's powers shall also be subject to any terms or supplemental or further terms agreed between the D&M Contractor and the Architect and incorporated into the document appointing the Adjudicator to act (which shall be based upon the form referred to in clause 36.3 of the D&M Contract).

20. GOVERNING LAW

This Agreement shall be governed by and interpreted in accordance with English law, and the D&M Contractor and the Architect hereby submit to the jurisdiction of the English Courts.

21. MISCELLANEOUS

21.1 Words importing the singular only shall also include the plural and vice versa, and where the context requires words importing persons shall include firms and corporations.

21.2 This Agreement supersedes any previous agreements or arrangements between the parties in respect of the services to be provided hereunder and represents the entire understanding between the parties in relation thereto.

21.3 Any notice to be served under this Agreement shall be served personally, by facsimile transmission, by telex or by first class pre-paid post. The addresses for service of the D&M Contractor and the Architect shall be those stated in this Agreement or such other address as the party to be served may have previously notified in writing. Any notice, if delivered personally, shall be deemed to have been served at the time of delivery or, if sent by facsimile transmission or by telex, shall be deemed to have been served at the time of transmission (but shall nevertheless be confirmed by first class pre-paid post) or, if sent by post, shall be deemed to have been served on the second business day following posting.

21.4 Nothing contained elsewhere in this Agreement shall in any way limit or exclude the D&M Contractor's rights and entitlements at common law or in equity to deduct or set-off any monies due to it by the Architect (whether by reason of the provisions of this Agreement or otherwise in consequence of any act, omission, default or breach of contract by the Architect in the performance of his obligations under this Agreement) from or against any sums otherwise due to the Architect under this Agreement.

EITHER
[21.5 The term "Architect" includes any additional partners who may be admitted into the partnership of the Architect during the currency of this Agreement. This Agreement shall not automatically terminate upon the death, retirement or resignation of any partner in the Architect, and the rights, obligations and liabilities of the partners in the Architect are joint and several.]

OR
[21.5 The Architect shall deliver to the D&M Contractor upon the execution of this Agreement a guarantee of his obligations and liabilities hereunder duly executed under seal by [the Architect's ultimate holding company/the directors for the time being of the Architect] in the form set out in the [Sixth] Schedule, and the D&M Contractor shall not be liable to make any payment under this Agreement until the Architect has complied with this clause.]

IN WITNESS whereof the D&M Contractor and [all the partners in] the Architect have executed this Agreement as a deed on the date first before written.

FIRST SCHEDULE TO D&M CONTRACTOR'S APPOINTMENT
A. The Architect's personnel referred to in clause 8.1 are:
. . . .

B. Details of minimum required professional indemnity cover (see clause 10.1):-

- ☐ Policy number: . . . .
- ☐ Expiry date: . . . .
- ☐ Limit of indemnity: . . . .
- ☐ Policy excess: . . . .
- ☐ Underwriters: . . . .
- ☐ Brokers: . . . .
- ☐ Minimum requirements of the D&M Contractor (which may be reviewed by the D&M Contractor): . . . .
  . . . .

Details of minimum required public liability cover (see clause 10.1):-

- ☐ Policy number: . . . .
- ☐ Expiry date: . . . .
- ☐ Limit of indemnity: . . . .
- ☐ Policy excess: . . . .
- ☐ Underwriters: . . . .

☐ Brokers: ....

☐ Minimum requirements of the D&M Contractor (which may be reviewed by the D&M Contractor): ....

....

SECOND SCHEDULE TO D&M CONTRACTOR'S APPOINTMENT: SCOPE OF SERVICES

The Services to be performed by the Architect as may be necessary or required by the D&M Contractor:-

[To be inserted]

THIRD SCHEDULE TO D&M CONTRACTOR'S APPOINTMENT: REMUNERATION AND TERMS OF PAYMENT

1. The fee payable to the Architect for all services to be provided under this Agreement (other than any Additional Services for which the Architect is entitled to receive additional payment) shall be an amount equal to [   ] per cent of the balance of the Final Prime Cost (after deducting all amounts payable to the Architect under this Agreement and all other Sub-Consultants less any payments made by the Employer under the Appointment after disregarding any sums paid thereunder for the preparation of the Employer's Requirements, the provision of Additional Services and the reimbursement of expenses and disbursements.

2. The reimbursable expenses and disbursements are net costs properly incurred by the Architect, as substantitated by invoices, vouchers and other documents to the reasonable satisfaction of the D&M Contractor, in respect of the following expenses and disbursements (if previously authorised or requested in writing by the D&M Contractor):-

2.1 reasonable hotel bills;

2.2 international travel and reasonable subsistence costs overseas;

2.3 models; and

2.4 printing costs for reports and tender documentation.

3. The D&M Contractor shall in accordance with the D&M Contract from time to time provide such information to the Employer's Representative as will enable the Employer's Representative to include in each interim certificate to be issued under the D&M Contract an amount which at the date thereof represents the total value of the services referred to in paragraph 1 above properly carried out by the Architect in accordance with this Agreement and the value of any reimbursable expenses and disbursements incurred by the Architect which may be included in interim certificates issued under the D&M Contract. The Architect shall provide such information as is required by the D&M Contractor for this purpose by the dates required by the D&M Contractor.

4. Within 21 Days of receipt by the D&M Contractor from the Employer's Representative of any interim certificate under the D&M Contract which includes an amount stated as due in respect of services performed by the Architect and any reimbursable expenses and disbursements referred to in paragraph 2 above, the D&M Contractor shall notify and pay to the

Architect the total value certified therein in respect of such services and reimbursable expenses and disbursements, less retention money, discount and all amounts previously paid to the Architect, and less any sum or sums which the Architect is liable to pay or allow to the D&M Contractor under this Agreement.

5. The D&M Contractor may retain from each amount payable to the Architect under paragraph 4 above prior to Practical Completion of the final Section of the Works a percentage at the rate specified in Schedule 1 of the D&M Contract. The amount so retained shall be subject to the following:-

5.1 the D&M Contractor's interest in any amount so retained shall be fiduciary as trustee for the Architect (but without obligation to invest), and the Architect's beneficial interest therein shall be subject only to the right of the D&M Contractor to have recourse thereto from time to time for payment of any amount which the D&M Contractor is entitled under the provisions of this Agreement or otherwise to deduct or set-off from any sum due to the Architect;

5.2 on the issue of the certificate of Practical Completion of the final Section of the Works under the D&M Contract one-half of the total amount then retained shall be released; and

5.3 on the issue of the Final Certificate under the D&M Contract the residue of the amount then retained shall be released.

6. The Architect shall co-operate fully with the D&M Contractor and the Employer's Representative in connection with any verification of applications for payment carried out by the Employer's Representative under the D&M Contract and, without prejudice to the generality of such obligation, shall provide to the Employer's Representative all such facilities and copies of documents as the Employer's Representative is entitled to call for under the D&M Contract (including all documents necessary for ascertaining the Final Prime Cost).

7. After the expiry of the Defects Liability Period in respect of the final Section of the Works, or, if later, after the issue of the Certificate of Making Good Defects in accordance with clause 20.4 of the D&M Contract, the Architect shall as soon as practicable prepare and submit to the D&M Contractor an account showing the difference between the amount due and payable to the Architect in accordance with paragraph 1 above and the amount previously paid on account thereof in accordance with paragraph 4 above. Such account shall be checked by the D&M Contractor, and the verified version thereof shall be included within its final account to be prepared and submitted to the Employer's Representative under the D&M Contract.

8. Immediately following the issue of the Final Certificate under the D&M Contract the D&M Contractor shall provide the Architect with a copy thereof and issue a certificate to the Architect stating the balance of any sums due to or from the D&M Contractor under this Agreement. All amounts stated in such certificate to be paid by the D&M Contractor to the Architect or by the Architect to the D&M Contractor (as the case may be) shall be paid within 30 Days of the issue of such certificate.

FOURTH SCHEDULE TO D&M CONTRACTOR'S APPOINTMENT:
D&M CONTRACT
[To be inserted]*

[FIFTH SCHEDULE TO D&M CONTRACTOR'S APPOINTMENT: LIST
OF PARTNERS]
[To be completed if appropriate]

[SIXTH SCHEDULE TO D&M CONTRACTOR'S APPOINTMENT:
DIRECTORS'/ULTIMATE HOLDING COMPANY GUARANTEE]
[To be inserted if appropriate]

SEVENTH SCHEDULE: FORM OF APPOINTMENT OF
ADJUDICATOR REFERRED TO IN CLAUSE 19.3
Dear
[. . . .]

On behalf of [. . . .] we are
pleased to confirm your appointment as Adjudicator for the Design and
Management Agreement between [. . . .]
and [. . . .] and for all Trade
Contracts and terms of engagement between [. . . .
. . . .] or [. . . .] and the
duly appointed Trade Contractors and professional consultants.

The following conditions will be deemed by all parties to the agreements
referred to above to constitute part of the terms of appointment of the
Adjudicator:-

1. The Adjudicator to be named in such agreements will be:-
. . . .
The address for all communications with regard to the Adjudicator's role
will be:-
. . . .

2. No dispute or difference referred to the Adjudicator under clause 36 of
the Design and Management Agreement and/or under clause 34 of any of
the Trade Contracts and/or under the professional consultants' agreements
will include matters of time and cost in the same submission. The
Adjudicator shall rule separately on such matters, even if related to the
same dispute or difference.

3. The parties to each such agreement shall indemnify the Adjudicator from
and against any claim of negligence in connection with his determinations
on disputes or differences.

4. The Adjudicator will give reasonable notice to the Employer's
Representative if he is unavailable for consultation. In the event of the
Adjudicator's temporary unavailability, disputes or differences will be held
pending for seven Days before the provisions of clause 36.4 of the Design

---

* See Appendix 2 of this book for an explanatory memorandum summarising the
D&M Contract.

and Management Agreement, clause 34 of the Trade Contract and clause 19.4 of the professional consultants' agreements are invoked.

5. The fees for the services of the Adjudicator will be as set out below:-

5.1 A lump sum Retaining Fee of [£ . . . . . .] will be paid by [. . . . .] to the Adjudicator for holding himself available until [. . . . .], for appraising himself of the terms and conditions of the Design and Management Agreement and of each Trade Contract and professional consultant's agreement and their ancillary documentation, for tendering advice on matters within the competence of the Adjudicator if so requested by the parties, for visiting the Site from time to time (by appointment) and generally for accepting the responsibilities of the Adjudicator under the Design and Management Agreement, the Trade Contracts and the professional consultants' agreements.

5.2 If it is agreed that the services of the Adjudicator shall be extended beyond [. . . . .] for any reason, an additional lump sum Retaining Fee of [£ . . . . . .] per month will be paid by [. . . . .] to the Adjudicator.

5.3 In the event of disputes or differences arising which require settlement by the Adjudicator, the Adjudicator will be paid an hourly fee of [£ . . . . . .] in addition to the aforementioned Retaining Fee. As part of his determination of such disputes or differences the Adjudicator shall determine which party shall bear the cost of such hourly fee or in which proportions such fee shall be borne by the parties.

6. Fees paid to the Adjudicator will not form part of the Prime Cost.

7. The appointment of the Adjudicator under any agreement may be determined at any time by notice in writing signed by the parties thereto (and by [. . . . .], if not a party thereto). If the appointment of the Adjudicator is so determined under all agreements relating to the project no further fees will be payable to the Adjudicator other than fees accrued due at the date of the final such determination.

Yours faithfully

[EIGHTH SCHEDULE: LIST OF PARTNERS]
[To be completed if appropriate]

[NINTH SCHEDULE: DIRECTORS'/ULTIMATE HOLDING COMPANY GUARANTEE]
[To be inserted if appropriate]

Appendix 2: Explanatory memorandum summarising the proposed d&m contractor's agreement

[A guaranteed maximum price is not employed in this example. The example is for a shell and core development with an option to fit out.]

This Explanatory Memorandum is not a Contract Document and is written to provide guidance only to the full Contract documentation. Accordingly, while this Explanatory Memorandum is believed to be an accurate summary of the terms of the proposed Design and Management Agreement, no responsibility can be accepted for any omissions or inaccuracies.

For convenience of use, copies of the Contents pages from the proposed Design and Management Agreement are attached at the end of the Explanatory Memorandum.

Parties – (1) [. . . . .] Ltd ("the Employer") and (2) the Design and Management Contractor ("the D&M Contractor").

RECITALS

(A) – Definitions of the Works, the Brief and the Site. The Works consist of the demolition of the existing building, the design and construction of a new 14-storey office building (with some retail areas at street level) *("the Basic Works")* and, if the Employer so elects, the design and construction therein of certain fitting-out works *("the Landlord's Works")*.

(B) – The Brief has been prepared by the Employer's Professional Team, who will continue to advise the Employer throughout the project. The D&M Contractor will however also engage certain members of the Professional Team to carry out the detailed design of the Works.

(C) – The Employer will employ the D&M Contractor initially to provide preliminary advice and assistance during the Pre- Construction Stage. If the Employer chooses to proceed with the same D&M Contractor during the Construction Stage the D&M Contractor will then complete the detailed design of the Works and procure, manage, organise and continually supervise the construction of the Works.

(D) – The completed development is intended to be let to one or more Tenants.

(E) – The Employer is a "contractor" for the purposes of the Statutory Tax Deduction Scheme.

1. DEFINITIONS AND INTERPRETATION
1.1 Definitions.

1.2 Clause numbers, etc. relate to this Agreement unless otherwise stated.

1.3 Statutory references include amended, re-enacted or subordinate legislation.

1.4 Headings shall not affect the construction or interpretation of this Agreement.

1.5 The singular shall include the plural, etc.

1.6 No consent or approval by the Employer, the Employer's Representative or the Professional Team shall relieve the D&M Contractor of any of its liabilities or obligations under this Agreement.

2. SCOPE OF AGREEMENT
2.1 The D&M Contractor's obligations during the Pre-Construction Stage shall be to co-operate with the Professional Team in relation to outline design, planning, programming, cost estimating and general organisation of the Works, to agree the Employer's Requirements, the Construction Programme and the Target Cost and to assist in arranging the placing of early orders for materials and otherwise.

2.2 If the Employer continues the employment of the D&M Contractor for the Construction Stage the D&M Contractor's obligations shall be to complete or procure the completion of the detailed design and to procure, manage, organise and continually supervise the design and construction of the Works. In so doing the D&M Contractor shall employ certain members of the Professional Team as Sub-Consultants, shall assume (by novation) any Pre-Ordered Trade Contract Packages let by the Employer during the Pre-Construction Stage, shall enter into Trade Contracts for the remainder of the Works and shall provide certain other general services and facilities as referred to in *Clause 10*.

3. PARENT COMPANY GUARANTEE
3.1 The D&M Contractor shall provide a guarantee from its ultimate holding company in the form set out in *Annex A*.

4. DIRECT AGREEMENTS BY TRADE CONTRACTORS, SUB-CONSULTANTS AND THE D&M CONTRACTOR
4.1 The D&M Contractor shall procure that each Trade Contractor shall enter into Warranty Agreements under seal with the Employer (in the form set out in *Annex B*) and with any company or institution providing finance for the Works or any part thereof or with any purchaser or mortgagee of the Site or the completed Works or any part thereof or with any or all of the Tenants (in the form set out in *Annex C*).

4.2 The D&M Contractor shall procure Warranty Agreements under seal in favour of the same beneficiaries from each Sub-Consultant (other than those originally engaged by the Employer) in the form set out in *Annexes D and E*.

4.3 The D&M Contractor shall itself enter into Warranty Agreements under seal (in the form set out in *Annex F*) with any company or institution providing finance for the Works or any part thereof or with any purchaser, mortgagee or Tenant as aforesaid.

4.4 All such Warranty Agreements shall be delivered to the Employer's Representative within 14 days of the relevant appointment or of his written notice.

5. EMPLOYER'S OBLIGATIONS

5.1 The Employer's obligations during the Pre-Construction Stage shall be as set out in *Clauses 5.1.1* to *5.1.6*, as follows:

5.1.1 To provide the services of the Employer's Representative and the other members of the Professional Team to assist and co-operate with the D&M Contractor generally.

5.1.2 To provide the D&M Contractor with such information as may reasonably be required.

5.1.3 After consultation with the D&M Contractor, to place agreed Pre-Ordered Trade Contract Packages on the terms of the pro forma Trade Contract set out in *Appendix C*.

5.1.4 To make all payments falling due under such Pre-Ordered Trade Contract Packages during the Pre-Construction Stage (such payments to form part of the Prime Cost).

5.1.5 To insure materials and equipment delivered under Pre-Ordered Trade Contract Packages for their full replacement value.

5.1.6 If full-scale mock-ups are required, to provide suitable premises therefor at the Employer's cost.

6. D&M CONTRACTOR'S OBLIGATIONS

6.1 The D&M Contractor's obligations during the Pre-Construction Stage shall be as set out in *Clauses 6.1.1* to *6.1.6*, as follows, in each case exercising all the reasonable skill, care and diligence of a suitably qualified and experienced contractor:

6.1.1 To advise and assist in relation to the planning and organisation of preparations for the Works, including without limitation the specific services listed in *Schedule 3 Part A*, and to assist and co-operate in the drawing up of the Employer's Requirements, the Construction Programme and the Target Cost, all in accordance with the Pre-Construction Programme. Such Construction Programme will provide for an overall construction period not exceeding [. . .] weeks. The Target Cost will include a fixed sum for preliminaries and will generally conform to and not exceed the Anticipated Target Cost included in the Brief.

6.1.2 To manage the project with a designated and suitably qualified Project Manager, together with all necessary supporting staff. The named Project Manager and key supporting staff shall not be changed without the Employer's consent. The Employer's Representative may at any time reasonably require the replacement of the Project Manager or any other supporting staff.

6.1.3 To assist and co-operate with the Employer's Representative in relation to Pre-Ordered Trade Contract Packages.

6.1.4 To inspect and manage the storage of materials and equipment delivered under the Pre-Ordered Trade Contract Packages, but with title thereto remaining at all times in the Employer.

6.1.5 To comply with all instructions and directions of the Employer's Representative.

6.1.6 To adhere to the Budget, so that no change is made without the sanction of the Employer's Representative.

7. PRE-CONSTRUCTION STAGE FEE

7.1 The Pre-Construction Stage Fee shall be a fixed lump sum payable in equal monthly instalments on or before the 14th day of the month following the month to which the relevant payment relates. If the Pre-Construction Stage is extended for any reason not attributable to the D&M Contractor additional monthly payments of the same amount will be payable.

8. COMPLETION OF PRE-CONSTRUCTION STAGE

8.1 Within 14 days after finalisation of the Employer's Requirements, the Construction Programme and the Target Cost and after notification from the Employer's Representative of the date when it will be practicable to commence the Construction Stage the Employer will notify the D&M Contractor whether its employment is to continue during the Construction Stage.

8.2 If the D&M Contractor's employment is not to continue, then the Employer shall pay to the D&M Contractor any part of the Pre-Construction Stage Fee then remaining unpaid.

8.3 If the D&M Contractor's employment is to continue, then the D&M Contractor shall commence carrying out the services required during the Construction Stage, shall enter into Sub-Consultants' Agreements with the Architect, the Structural Engineer and the M&E Consultant in the form set out in *Appendices D, E and F,* shall enter into any further necessary Sub-Consultants' Agreements, shall enter into novations of the Pre-Ordered Trade Contract Packages and shall thereafter ensure the regular and diligent progress of the design and construction of the Works and the completion of each Section on or before the relevant Completion Date.

8.4 The Employer may terminate the D&M Contractor's employment at any time during the Pre-Construction Stage and pay the D&M Contractor a proportionate part of the Pre- Construction Stage Fee.

8.5 In the event of termination the D&M Contractor shall deliver all preliminary drawings, designs, etc. to the Employer's Representative. Such materials shall be subject to the copyright licence detailed in *Clause 33.*

8.6 Termination payments under *Clause 8.2* or *8.4* shall represent the full extent of the D&M Contractor's entitlement to compensation and shall be without prejudice to any rights or remedies of the Employer in respect of prior breaches.

9. EMPLOYER'S OBLIGATIONS IN THE CONSTRUCTION STAGE
9.1 The Employer's obligations during the Construction Stage shall be as set out in *Clauses 9.1.1* to *9.1.4*, as follows:

9.1.1 To give possession of the Site to the D&M Contractor.

9.1.2 To continue to provide the services of the Employer's Representative to co-operate with the D&M Contractor generally.

9.1.3 To continue to provide such information and instructions as may be reasonably required.

9.1.4 To novate to the D&M Contractor all Pre-Ordered Trade Contract Packages.

10. D&M CONTRACTOR'S OBLIGATIONS IN THE CONSTRUCTION STAGE
10.1 The D&M Contractor's obligations during the Construction Stage shall be as set out in *Clauses 10.1.1* to *10.1.11*, as follows, all in accordance with the Construction Programme:-

10.1.1 To complete or procure the completion of the detailed design of the Basic Works.

10.1.2 To procure, manage, organise and continually supervise the construction of the whole of the Works. The D&M Contractor shall be deemed to have investigated and satisfied itself as to relevant Site conditions and facilities so far as reasonably possible.

10.1.3 Without prejudice thereto, to provide the specific services and facilities listed in *Schedule 3 Part B* and, where appropriate, to continue to provide those listed in *Schedule 3 Part A*.

10.1.4 To continue to maintain its Project Manager and supporting staff.

10.1.5 To provide all reasonably required assistance to and co-operation with the Employer's Representative.

10.1.6 To comply or secure compliance with all instructions of the Employer's Representative.

10.1.7 To comply and to secure compliance by all Sub-Consultants and Trade Contractors with all relevant Statutory Requirements, all fees to be paid by the D&M Contractor and treated as items of Prime Cost. If as a result a variation in the Employer's Requirements is required the D&M Contractor shall give 14 days' notice before proceeding, during which the Employer's Representative may give specific instructions.

10.1.8 At all times to prevent any public or private nuisance or other interference with the rights of any adjoining or neighbouring landowner, tenant or occupier or any statutory undertaker, to assist the Employer in defending any relevant proceedings and to indemnify the Employer in respect thereof. Such indemnity shall not extend to any nuisance or interference which results from any variation or other instruction of the Employer's Representative (unless itself caused by the D&M Contractor or any Trade Contractor or Sub-Consultant) and which could not reasonably have been avoided by the D&M Contractor.

10.1.9 To ensure that there is no trespass on or over any adjoining or neighbouring property. The D&M Contractor shall obtain all necessary agreements with adjoining owners, including crane licences, on terms previously approved by the Employer.

10.1.10 To secure compliance by all Trade Contractors with any restrictions on working hours.

10.1.11 To continue to adhere and to secure adherence by all Trade Contractors and Sub-Consultants to the Budget, so that no change is made without the sanction of the Employer's Representative.

11. DESIGN

11.1 The D&M Contractor shall be responsible for all design work carried out by Trade Contractors, whether before or after the commencement of the Construction Stage, and for all design work produced by the Sub-Consultants during the Construction Stage. The D&M Contractor shall also be responsible for integrating such designs with the construction requirements of the Works, for ensuring buildability and for co-ordinating the carrying out of all such design work.

11.2 In respect of all design work which is its responsibility the D&M Contractor warrants that it will exercise all the skill, care and diligence to be expected of a suitably qualified and experienced consultant or contractor.

11.3 The D&M Contractor warrants that no deleterious goods or materials will be recommended or selected by or on behalf of the D&M Contractor or incorporated into the Works.

11.4 The D&M Contractor acknowledges that the Employer will be relying on the skill and judgement of the D&M Contractor, its Sub-Consultants and Trade Contractors in respect of their design and that the D&M Contractor shall accordingly be fully responsible therefor (unless the D&M Contractor shall have given the Employer express notice to the contrary).

11.5 In payment for such design work the Employer shall pay the D&M Contractor the Design Fee (as an item of Prime Cost), out of which the D&M Contractor shall pay all Sub-Consultants' fees. The Design Fee shall be the percentage of the Final Prime Cost (after deducting the Design Fee and any payments to Sub-Consultants) determined in accordance with *Schedule 2* and shall be paid by interim instalments calculated by reference to interim certificates.

11.6 The D&M Contractor shall be fully responsible for the design and co-ordination of all temporary works and shall indemnify the Employer in respect of any failure or inadequacy. *Clauses 14.3.2* (which limits the D&M Contractor's liability to the Employer to amounts recovered from Trade Contractors and Sub-Consultants) and *14.3.3* (which provides for reimbursement of the D&M Contractor's costs of enforcing its contractual rights against Trade Contractors and Sub-Consultants) shall not apply to any such liability.

12. EMPLOYMENT OF TRADE CONTRACTORS

12.1 The D&M Contractor shall accept novations of all Pre-Ordered Trade Contract Packages, shall indemnify the Employer against all liability to the relevant Trade Contractors and shall adopt and assume responsibility for all materials and equipment delivered during the Pre-Construction Stage.

12.2 The D&M Contractor shall agree with the Employer's Representative the most suitable division of the remainder of the Works into Trade Contract Packages and the most appropriate tenderers therefor, and the D&M Contractor shall then obtain fixed price tenders on the best available market terms. The D&M Contractor shall make recommendations to the Employer's Representative and, following consultations, the Employer's Representative shall instruct the D&M Contractor which tenders to accept.

12.3 The D&M Contractor shall promptly enter into Trade Contracts with the selected tenderers on the basis of the pro forma Trade Contract set out in *Appendix C*.

12.4 If the D&M Contractor is unable to reach agreement on the terms of the Trade Contract with any prospective Trade Contractor the D&M Contractor shall refer the matter to the Employer's Representative for further instructions.

12.5 Each Trade Contract shall so far as practicable be in the form set out in *Appendix C*, although the Employer may approve variations following consultations. All Trade Contracts shall as a minimum require the Trade Contractor to execute such Trade Contracts under seal, to provide the Warranty Agreements referred to in *Clause 4.1* above, to observe, perform and comply with the terms of this Agreement on a back-to-back basis, to indemnify the D&M Contractor against the same liabilities as arise under this Agreement, to indemnify the D&M Contractor against third party claims and obtain insurance in respect thereof, to complete the Trade Contract Package within the specified period or periods and to entitle the Employer to terminate the Trade Contractor's employment in the event of the determination of the D&M Contractor's employment under this Agreement.

12.6 The D&M Contractor shall not invite tenders from associated companies without first supplying full details to the Employer. Otherwise the Employer may require the D&M Contractor to terminate the relevant Trade Contract at the D&M Contractor's cost.

12.7 Subject to *Clause 14*, the D&M Contractor shall be fully responsible for all acts, omissions and defaults of its Trade Contractors as if they were its own acts, omissions and defaults.

13. ADMINISTRATION OF TRADE CONTRACTORS AND SUB-CONSULTANTS

13.1 The Employer's Representative shall inform the D&M Contractor how much has been included in each interim certificate in respect of each Trade

Contractor's works and Sub- Consultant's services. The D&M Contractor shall pay the relevant Trade Contractors and Sub-Consultants within 21 days of receipt of each interim certificate.

13.2 Before issuing any certificate the Employer's Representative may require reasonable proof that amounts included in previous certificates have been duly paid to the relevant Trade Contractors and Sub-Consultants. If the D&M Contractor fails to comply the Employer may make direct payments and deduct the same from sums due to the D&M Contractor.

13.3 The Employer and its representatives shall have a right of access to the workshops and other premises of each Trade Contractor.

13.4 The Employer shall be entitled to terminate the employment of any Trade Contractor or Sub-Consultant in the event of the determination of the D&M Contractor's employment under this Agreement.

13.5 The D&M Contractor shall not grant extensions of time to a Trade Contractor without the Employer's Representative's consent. Trade Contractors shall be fully liable to the D&M Contractor for the consequences of any delay in completing their Trade Contract Packages.

13.6 Neither the Employer nor the Employer's Representative shall have any liability to any Trade Contractor or Sub-Consultant.

13.7 All Trade Contractors and Sub-Consultants shall be appointed in sufficient time to enable the D&M Contractor to comply with the Construction Programme.

14. D&M CONTRACTOR'S LIABILITY REGARDING TRADE CONTRACTORS AND SUB-CONSULTANTS

14.1 The D&M Contractor shall be fully liable to the Employer for any breach of or non-compliance with this Agreement, including any breach or non-compliance caused by any Trade Contractor or Sub-Consultant. The rights and remedies of the Employer under this Agreement shall be without prejudice to any other rights or remedies the Employer may have. The Employer shall be deemed to have relied exclusively on the D&M Contractor's skill and judgement.

14.2 Subject to *Clause 11.6*, if and to the extent that the D&M Contractor is liable to the Employer for any loss, damage or expense which is caused by any breach or non- compliance by any Trade Contractor or Sub-Consultant of its obligations to the D&M Contractor, then and to such extent *Clause 14.3* shall apply.

14.3 In such event:

14.3.1 The D&M Contractor in consultation with the Employer shall enforce the terms of the relevant Trade Contract or Sub-Consultant's agreement (including by legal action if necessary), shall secure satisfactory completion of the Works (including by the engagement of further Trade Contractors or Sub- Consultants if necessary) and shall meet any consequential claims by other Trade Contractors or Sub-Consultants.

14.3.2 The Employer shall not be entitled to deduct, claim or recover from the D&M Contractor in respect of any breach or non-compliance any sums in excess of those, if any, which the D&M Contractor shall have recovered and received from the defaulting Trade Contractor or Sub-Consultant in respect thereof.

14.3.3 The Employer shall reimburse the D&M Contractor any irrecoverable expenditure properly incurred by the D&M Contractor in taking the steps referred to in *Clause 14.3.1.*

14.3.4 Unless the Employer otherwise agrees, the D&M Contractor will not be entitled to payment from the Employer of any sums in respect of any Trade Contract works or Sub- Consultant's services which have not been certified under this Agreement until such sums (including costs, if any) become payable to the Trade Contractor or Sub-Consultant by the D&M Contractor by reason of a final judgement against the D&M Contractor.

14.4 If a Trade Contractor or Sub-Consultant makes a claim against the D&M Contractor alleging a breach of the relevant Trade Contract or Sub-Consultant's agreement, then the D&M Contractor shall immediately inform the Employer's Representative and (subject to any instructions he may give) shall take all such action as may be necessary to settle or defend such claim and pay any amount due. The Employer shall reimburse the D&M Contractor its costs of settling or defending such claim to the extent that they shall have arisen from any negligence, default or breach of contract of the Employer or the Employer's Representative.

15. WORKS BY PERSONS OTHER THAN THE D&M CONTRACTOR, TRADE CONTRACTORS OR SUB-CONSULTANTS

15.1 The D&M Contractor shall permit contemporaneous work by persons employed or engaged by the Employer and/or by any Tenant, provided that in the case of fitting-out works to be carried out by Tenants ("Tenants' Fitting-Out Works") a certificate of Readiness for Fitting-Out shall have been issued in respect of the relevant Section. Following consultations with the D&M Contractor, the Employer's Representative shall issue an Access Regime Document setting out the procedures and conditions which shall apply to the carrying out of such work contemporaneously with the Basic Works or any Landlord's Works. The Employer shall use all reasonable endeavours to secure that such persons comply with any applicable Access Regime Document and with the D&M Contractor's reasonable safety requirements and shall indemnify the D&M Contractor against consequential claims for personal injury or damage to property.

15.2 The Employer's Representative shall be entitled to give reasonable directions to the D&M Contractor from time to time with regard to the regulation and co-ordination of such work.

16. MATERIALS, GOODS AND WORKMANSHIP

16.1 The D&M Contractor shall procure the provision of all necessary labour, materials, goods, plant, stores and services and shall be responsible for all materials and equipment delivered under Pre-Ordered Trade Contract Packages.

16.2 The D&M Contractor shall procure materials, goods and workmanship as required by the Employer's Requirements or otherwise in accordance with the Employer's Representative's reasonable instructions. The D&M Contractor shall retain all relevant vouchers and certificates and shall procure that the benefit of any manufacturer's or supplier's warranties is passed on to the Employer. The Employer's Representative shall be entitled to reject materials, goods or workmanship and require the D&M Contractor to replace and/or make good the same at the D&M Contractor's cost.

16.3 All materials, goods and workmanship shall be of at least a standard appropriate to the Works and shall be to the reasonable satisfaction of the Employer's Representative.

16.4 Unfixed materials and goods shall become the property of the Employer upon their delivery to or adjacent to the Site and shall not then be removed without the consent of the Employer's Representative.

16.5 Undelivered materials or goods shall only be included in an interim certificate at the discretion of the Employer's Representative and if the conditions of *Clause 28.4* are satisfied. If undelivered materials or goods are included they shall become the property of the Employer upon payment of the relevant certificate. The D&M Contractor shall then take all reasonable steps to protect the same.

17. CONTINGENCY, VARIATIONS AND ADDITIONAL WORKS

17.1 The Target Cost for the Basic Works will include a [two] per cent contingency to be expended by the D&M Contractor only with the prior approval of the Employer's Representative.

17.2 The Employer's Representative may issue instructions requiring variations to the content or timing of the Works or the expenditure of provisional sums or daywork allowances in Trade Contracts. The D&M Contractor shall not vary the Works or authorise any such expenditure without the prior approval of the Employer's Representative.

17.3 The Employer's Representative may require from the D&M Contractor cost and time estimates for proposed variations before instructing the D&M Contractor to proceed.

17.4 The D&M Contractor, with the prior approval of the Employer's Representative, shall make variations to the Works which correct design defects or inadequacies or, if circumstances so require, so as to substitute materials or workmanship. Any resulting increase in costs shall be borne by the D&M Contractor.

17.5 If the Employer shall decide or contract with Tenants to carry out any fitting-out works the Employer may elect either to carry out such works itself or to require the D&M Contractor to carry out such works. Any such works carried out by the D&M Contractor shall be referred to as "Landlord's Works" and shall be treated as variations to the Works under *Clause 17.2* and as separate Sections thereof. The Employer's Representative shall issue such further directions or instructions as may be appropriate.

18. ACCESS

18.1 The D&M Contractor shall provide the Employer's Representative and his representatives with access at all reasonable times to the Site and to the workshops or other premises of the D&M Contractor and its Trade Contractors.

19. COMMENCEMENT AND COMPLETION

19.1 The D&M Contractor shall procure the commencement of the Works on or by the Commencement Date, the regular and diligent progress and execution of the Works and the completion of each Section on the Date for Completion for that Section.

19.2 For insurance purposes the D&M Contractor shall retain possession of each Section until Practical Completion thereof.

19.3 After the issue of the certificate of Readiness for Fitting-Out of any Section the Employer and/or Tenants may use or occupy such Section or any part thereof. Until then the D&M Contractor's consent is required, such consent not to be unreasonably withheld.

19.4 Notwithstanding any such use or occupation by the Employer and/or Tenants, Practical Completion shall not be deemed to have taken place until the issue of the certificate of Practical Completion in respect of the relevant Section. Until then the D&M Contractor shall remain responsible for such Section and shall comply with all relevant insurance requirements.

20. READINESS FOR FITTING-OUT, PRACTICAL COMPLETION AND DEFECTS LIABILITY

20.1 The Employer's Representative shall issue certificates of Readiness for Fitting-Out for each Section when the D&M Contractor's works for that Section have been substantially completed so as to enable any fitting-out works to be commenced without any significant disruption.

20.2 The Employer's Representative shall issue certificates of Practical Completion for each Section, whereupon the Defects Liability Period shall commence. Plant and machinery supplied or installed as part of any Landlord's Works must first have been satisfactorily commissioned and tested by the Joint Commissioning Engineer. The D&M Contractor shall promptly make good any snagging items.

20.3 The Employer's Representative shall deliver a schedule of defects to the D&M Contractor within 28 days after the expiry of the Defects Liability Period. The D&M Contractor shall then make good such defects within 28 days of receipt thereof, unless the Employer's Representative otherwise instructs (in which event an appropriate deduction shall be made).

20.4 The Employer's Representative shall issue a certificate of making good defects when all defects have been made good.

20.5 If so requested by the Employer, the D&M Contractor shall then assign to the Employer any rights in respect of defects arising under any Trade Contracts.

21. EXTENSIONS OF TIME AND DELAY

21.1 The D&M Contractor shall forthwith give the Employer's Representative notice of any delays together with its assessment of any consequent adjustment to the Target Cost. The Employer's Representative shall as soon as practicable notify the D&M Contractor of the extension of time, if any, which he considers fair and reasonable, provided the D&M Contractor constantly uses its best endeavours to minimise the delay. The Employer's Representative may subsequently revise any such extension of time but shall not fix a Completion Date earlier than the Date for Completion unless work has been omitted.

21.2 The grounds for extensions of time are delays caused by defaults of the Employer or its representatives, instructions of the Employer's Representative or events entitling Trade Contractors to extensions of time under their Trade Contracts (except when arising from failures by other Trade Contractors). Delays caused by the negligence, default or breach of contract of the D&M Contractor or any Trade Contractor or Sub-Consultant are excluded.

21.3 The D&M Contractor shall assist the Employer's Representative in determining any entitlement to an extension of time.

21.4 The Employer's Representative shall certify any delay in procuring Practical Completion of any Section. Liquidated damages shall be payable at the rate stated in *Schedule 1* (or, for any Landlord's Works, at such rate as may be agreed).

22. INJURY TO PERSONS AND PROPERTY – INSURANCE AND INDEMNITY

22.1 The D&M Contractor and its Trade Contractors shall keep the Employer indemnified and insured against third party personal injury and damage to property claims, except to the extent due to any act or neglect of the Employer or its agents. Damage to property does not include damage to the Works or to unfixed materials or goods.

22.2 The D&M Contractor and its Trade Contractors shall maintain adequate employer's liability insurance, with the Employer and the D&M Contractor indemnified as joint insureds.

22.3 The amount of the insurance cover required under *Clauses 22.1 and 22.2* shall be not less than as stated in *Schedule 1*.

22.4 The D&M Contractor and its Trade Contractors shall produce copy policies and premium receipts when required.

22.5 If the D&M Contractor or any Trade Contractor fails to insure the Employer may itself do so and recover the premium from the D&M Contractor.

23. INSURANCE OF THE WORKS

23.1 The Employer shall maintain a project insurance policy in the joint names of itself, the D&M Contractor and all Trade Contractors. The D&M Contractor and its Trade Contractors shall strictly observe and comply with all relevant conditions and requirements, and the D&M Contractor shall immediately notify the Employer's Representative of any matter which may affect the policy.

23.2 The Employer shall produce evidence of and receipts for such policy as and when reasonably requested by the D&M Contractor.

23.3 If a likely claims situation arises the D&M Contractor shall immediately give notice thereof to the Employer's Representative, provide him with completed claim forms and all such further information and assistance as he may reasonably require and take all reasonable steps to reduce or prevent any further loss or damage.

23.4 Save as provided in this Agreement, loss or damage to the Works or to unfixed materials or goods shall be disregarded in calculating the amounts payable to the D&M Contractor under this Agreement.

23.5 All deductibles under such policy shall be included as items within the Prime Cost.

24. D&M CONTRACTOR'S, TRADE CONTRACTORS' AND SUB-CONSULTANTS' INSURANCES

24.1 The D&M Contractor and its Trade Contractors shall insure for their full value all materials and goods prior to their delivery to the Site and all contractors' plant, tools, equipment and temporary buildings.

24.2 The Employer's Representative may require the D&M Contractor to oblige any Trade Contractor to effect and maintain additional joint names insurance of the Works or any unfixed goods or materials up to the value of the deductibles under the project insurance policy.

24.3 The D&M Contractor shall obtain the prior approval of the Employer's insurance advisers to the policies referred to in *Clauses 24.1. and 24.2*, comply with all reasonable requirements of the Employer's Representative in relation thereto and provide evidence thereof and receipts therefor when required.

24.4 The D&M Contractor shall procure that all Sub-Consultants maintain appropriate professional indemnity policies and provide evidence thereof when required. No actual, anticipated or potential claims thereunder shall be settled, waived or compromised without the Employer's Representative's consent.

25. REGARDING INSURANCE GENERALLY

25.1 All D&M Contractor's insurances under *Clauses 22* and *24* shall be effected with insurers previously approved by the Employer's Representative.

25.2 After any inspection required by the insurers has been completed the D&M Contractor shall with due diligence make good any loss or damage to the Works or to any unfixed materials or goods. Such work shall be treated as if it were a variation under *Clause 17.2*, and the Employer's Representative may issue such further directions or instructions as he considers appropriate.

25.3 All insurance monies shall be paid to the Employer, who shall pass on such monies to the D&M Contractor against interim certificates as the restoration work proceeds. If and to the extent that the loss and damage was caused by any negligence, default or breach of contract of the D&M Contractor or any Trade Contractor or Sub-Consultant the D&M Contractor shall not be entitled to any payment for such restoration of work beyond such insurance monies.

26. DETERMINATION BY THE EMPLOYER

26.1 The Employer may forthwith determine the D&M Contractor's employment by notice at any time.

26.2 If such determination does not arise from any of the matters stated in *Clause 26.3* the Employer shall pay to the D&M Contractor in full settlement the Prime Cost of work carried out and materials supplied and of any further expenditure reasonably and irrevocably incurred by reason of previous instructions of the Employer's Representative and an appropriate proportion of the Construction Stage Fee.

26.3 If such determination arises from default or insolvency of the D&M Contractor the rights and duties of the Employer and the D&M Contractor shall be as provided in *Clause 26.4*.

26.4 In such event the D&M Contractor shall allow or pay to the Employer any expense and direct loss and/or damage caused by the determination. The Employer shall not be bound to make any further payment to the D&M Contractor until after completion of the Works, whereupon the Employer's Representative shall certify such expense, loss and/or damage. The appropriate net payment shall then be made to the Employer by the D&M Contractor or vice versa.

26.5 Upon a determination of the D&M Contractor's employment under *Clause 26 or 27* the Employer may employ others to complete the work using the D&M Contractor's temporary buildings, plant, tools, equipment, goods and materials. If so required, the D&M Contractor shall assign or novate all relevant supply contracts, plant hire agreements or other relevant contracts. The D&M Contractor shall deliver possession of the Site to the Employer, and when so required (but not before) shall remove from the Works its temporary buildings, plant, tools, equipment, goods and materials, failing which the Employer's Representative may remove and sell the same and hold the proceeds (less costs) to the credit of the D&M Contractor. The D&M Contractor shall promptly deliver to the Employer's Representative all models, mock-ups and documentation relating to the Works, whether or not completed.

27. DETERMINATION BY THE D&M CONTRACTOR

The D&M Contractor may terminate its employment (in which event the Employer shall pay the D&M Contractor the amounts referred to in *Clause 26.2* in full settlement, and the provisions of *Clause 26.5* shall apply) in the event of:

27.1 The Employer's Representative unreasonably withholding the issue of a certificate for 14 days after receipt of written notice of default.

27.2 The Employer not paying the D&M Contractor any sums certified by the Employer's Representative within 14 days after receipt of written notice of default.

27.3 The insolvency of the Employer.

27.4 The suspension of the Works under the specific instruction of the Employer or any court of law or other competent authority for a continuous period exceeding 12 weeks.

27.5 The suspension of the Works for a continuous period exceeding 12 weeks following written notice from the D&M Contractor that the Employer or the Employer's Representative is preventing the regular and proper execution of the Works.

27.6 The Employer interfering with or obstructing the issue of any certificate.

28. PAYMENT
28.1 The Employer shall pay the D&M Contractor the Final Prime Cost and the Construction Stage Fee in full payment for the performance of the D&M Contractor's obligations during the Construction Stage.

The Final Prime Cost shall include the Pre-Construction Stage Fee (other than an overhead and profit allowance of [.....%] and monies actually expended during the Pre-Construction and Construction Stages on the items referred to in *Schedule 4 Part A*, but shall exclude the items referred to in *Schedule 4 Part B*.

Such included items are certain Sub-Consultants' disbursements, the Design Fee, the D&M Contractor's staff and labour costs, the cost of materials and goods provided or adopted by the D&M Contractor, the cost of plant, consumable stores and services provided by the D&M Contractor, insurance and other sundry costs incurred by the D&M Contractor and amounts payable by the D&M Contractor to Trade Contractors (but after deducting discounts, amounts payable by reason of defaults of the D&M Contractor or any Trade Contractor or Sub-Consultant and any amounts deducted or recovered by the D&M Contractor from any other Trade Contractor or from any Sub-Consultant).

Such excluded items are items specifically stated not to be recoverable, excessive or unreasonable costs, costs or additional costs incurred by reason of default or negligence, any fees payable to Sub-Consultants in excess of the Design Fee, any item included in the Construction Stage Fee and any costs incurred after Practical Completion without the consent of the Employer's Representative.

The Construction Stage Fee shall be a percentage of the Final Prime Cost to be determined in accordance with Schedule 2, which states the anticipated percentage rate and contains a formula for adjusting such rate upwards or downwards on the basis that the fee implications of significant cost savings or cost overruns shall, within specified limits, be shared equally between the Employer and the D&M Contractor. A diagrammatic illustration of such adjustment provisions is attached at the end of this Explanatory Memorandum.*

28.2 The D&M Contractor shall submit monthly payment applications to the Employer's Representative together with such further documentation

* See Figure 11 of this book.

and facilities as he may reasonably require to verify such applications. The Employer's Representative shall verify or amend the amount applied for and issue an interim certificate for payment within 21 days, together if appropriate with a statement regarding any amounts disallowed. The Employer shall pay the D&M Contractor the amount due within 14 days after the date of the interim certificate or within seven days of receipt of an appropriate VAT invoice, whichever is the later.

28.3 The amount certified due shall be the total Prime Cost of work properly executed and materials and goods delivered to the Site (including the Design Fee), together with a proportionate part of the Construction Stage Fee, but less retention and any amounts previously paid.

28.4 The Employer's Representative may at its discretion include in interim certificates the value of materials and goods not yet delivered to the Site (but not the Construction Stage Fee or the Design Fee thereon) provided certain detailed conditions set out in this clause are complied with.

28.5 Retentions shall be deducted from items of Prime Cost (excluding the Design Fee and amounts paid to Sub-Consultants) at the rate specified in *Schedule 1*. The Employer shall hold such retentions on trust (but without obligation to invest). One half of such retentions shall be released on the issue of the certificate of Practical Completion for the relevant Section and the balance shall be released on the issue of the Final Certificate.

28.6 The D&M Contractor shall provide the Employer's Representative with all documents necessary to ascertain the Final Prime Cost not later than six months after Practical Completion of the final Section. After the expiry of the Defects Liability Period in respect of such Section (or the issue of the certificate of making good defects) the D&M Contractor shall submit to the Employer's Representative its final account showing the final balance due to or from the Employer.

28.7 Within three months of receipt of the D&M Contractor's final account the Employer's Representative shall verify the total Final Prime Cost and Construction Stage Fee and determine any change of rate for the Construction Stage Fee in accordance with *Schedule 2*. The D&M Contractor shall provide the Employer's Representative with all reasonable facilities and copy documents and shall procure the like facilities and copy documents from Trade Contractors and Sub-Consultants.

28.8 Not later than four months after the date of submission of the D&M Contractor's final account the Employer's Representative shall issue the Final Certificate showing the final balance due to or from the D&M Contractor under this Agreement. Such balance shall be paid within 28 days of the issue of the Final Certificate or within seven days of receipt of an appropriate VAT invoice, whichever is the later.

28.9 Unless either the Employer or the D&M Contractor gives notice of objection within 30 days after the issue of the Final Certificate, and then applies to the High Court within a further 30 days, the Final Certificate shall be conclusive evidence of such computations and of the final amount due.

28.10 Early final payment may be made to any Trade Contractor at the Employer's Representative's discretion if the Employer's Representative and the D&M Contractor so desire and if such Trade Contractor has satisfactorily indemnified the D&M Contractor against any latent defects and has provided all the Warranty Agreements required from it as at that date.

28.11 The Employer's Representative may at his discretion make interim adjustments to the rate of the Construction Stage Fee based on estimates of the Final Prime Cost and of the then Adjusted Target Cost, and future payments shall then be adjusted accordingly. The amount of any such adjustments shall be taken into account when the final account is calculated.

29. ADJUSTMENT OF TARGET COST

29.1 Either the Employer or the D&M Contractor may apply to the Employer's Representative for adjustment of the Target Cost at any time during the Construction Stage. The Employer's Representative shall be provided with all necessary information and facilities to evaluate the application.

29.2 The Employer's Representative shall notify the Employer and the D&M Contractor of any adjustment, upwards or downwards, which he considers fair and reasonable within 14 days of receipt of the application or of any further supporting information that he may have required. Any adjustment is conditional upon the D&M Contractor having used its best endeavours to avoid or mitigate the consequences of the event giving rise to the application.

29.3 The events which may give rise to an adjustment are variations, changes in Statutory Requirements (excluding those which Trade Contractors should have allowed for), events entitling the D&M Contractor to an extension of time under *Clause 21.2* and any expenditure of provisional sums in Trade Contracts.

30. STATUTORY TAX DEDUCTION SCHEME

30.1 to 30.9 These provisions relating to the operation of the Statutory Tax Deduction Scheme follow the usual JCT provisions.

31. VAT – SUPPLEMENTAL PROVISIONS

31.1 The VAT Agreement is set out in *Schedule 5*.

31.2 The Prime Cost, the Pre-Construction Stage Fee and the Construction Stage Fee are exclusive of VAT, which shall be chargeable in accordance with applicable legislation and with the VAT Agreement (which follows the usual JCT form, except that payments will only be made by the Employer against VAT invoices rather than authenticated receipts).

31.3 If the supply of goods and services to the Employer becomes exempt from tax the D&M Contractor shall be reimbursed the resulting loss of input tax.

32. SET-OFF

32.1 Nothing in this Agreement shall limit or exclude the Employer's rights of deduction or set-off.

33. COPYRIGHT AND CONFIDENTIALITY

33.1 Copyright in documents and materials will be retained by the D&M Contractor or by the relevant Trade Contractors or Sub-Consultants, but the Employer shall be granted a royalty-free, irrevocable and non-exclusive licence to use and reproduce such documents and materials for all purposes relating to the Works or the completed Works.

33.2 All documents and information shall be treated as confidential and not disclosed to third parties who do not require them unless the Employer's Representative otherwise instructs.

34. OBJECTS OF INTEREST OR VALUE

34.1 All objects found on Site shall become the property of the Employer. The D&M Contractor shall use its best endeavours not to disturb such objects, cease work if appropriate, take all the necessary steps to preserve such objects where they are found and inform the Employer's Representative.

34.2 The Employer's Representative shall issue instructions regarding such objects. These may require the D&M Contractor to permit the examination, excavation or removal of such objects by a third party (for whom the Employer shall be deemed responsible).

34.3 Additional costs incurred by the D&M Contractor shall be included as an item within the Prime Cost.

35. ASSIGNMENT AND SUB-LETTING

35.1 The Employer's consent is required to any assignment by the D&M Contractor of this Agreement or of any Trade Contract or Sub-Consultant's agreement and to any sub-letting of any of the D&M Contractor's management obligations.

35.2 The Employer may novate or assign to any company or institution providing finance for the Works or any part thereof or to any purchaser or mortgagee or to any Tenant or to any subsidiary or holding company of the Employer but shall not otherwise novate or assign without the D&M Contractor's consent.

36. SETTLEMENT OF DISPUTES

36.1 The Adjudicator shall be named in *Schedule 1*.

36.2 All disputes arising prior to Practical Completion of the final Section with regard to the D&M Contractor's entitlement to extensions of time, the exclusion of any item from the Prime Cost, any adjustment of the Target Cost, the Employer's right to terminate under *Clause 26.3* or the D&M Contractor's right to terminate under *Clause 27* shall be referred by either party to the Adjudicator, who shall give his decision within seven days. Each of such areas of dispute shall be treated as a separate reference. No such reference shall relieve either party from the performance of its obligations. The Adjudicator shall be entitled only to decide in favour of one or other of the parties and shall not be empowered to give a compromise decision unless both parties otherwise agree. The Adjudicator shall determine which party shall bear the costs of the reference, which shall be paid within 30 days of his decision.

36.3 The Adjudicator shall act as an expert and not as an arbitrator. His decision shall be final and binding until Practical Completion of the final Section. The Adjudicator's appointment shall be based upon the form set out in *Annex I*, which may also include other agreed terms.

36.4 If the Adjudicator fails to give his decision or is unable or refuses to act the dispute shall be referred to a substitute Adjudicator agreed between the parties or, failing agreement, appointed by the Chairman of the Chartered Institute of Arbitrators.

36.5 If the substitute Adjudicator refuses or neglects to give a decision or if either party is dissatisfied with the decision given by the Adjudicator or substitute Adjudicator such party may within 30 days give notice of its intention to refer the matter to the High Court for final determination. If no such notice is given within 30 days the Adjudicator's or substitute Adjudicator's decision shall remain final and binding.

36.6 All disputes which have not become final and binding under *Clause 36.5* and all other disputes relating to this Agreement or the project shall be referred to the High Court to be tried by a Judge sitting as such and not as an arbitrator. Unless the parties otherwise agree, no such reference shall be made until after Practical Completion of the final Section or the termination or alleged termination of the D&M Contractor's employment.

36.7 The Judge shall have full power to open up, review and revise all decisions, certificates, etc. of the Employer's Representative (except matters expressly left to his discretion) or of the Adjudicator or substitute Adjudicator and to direct such measurements and/or valuations as he considers desirable.

37. GOVERNING LAW
37.1 This Agreement shall be governed by English law, and the parties submit to the jurisdiction of the English Courts.

CONTENTS OF THE PROPOSED D&M CONTRACTOR'S AGREEMENT

CLAUSES
1. Definitions and interpretation
2. Scope of agreement
3. Parent company guarantee
4. Direct agreements by Trade Contractors, Sub-Consultants and the D&M Contractor
5. Employer's obligations
6. D&M Contractor's obligations
7. Pre-Construction Stage Fee
8. Completion of Pre-Construction Stage
9. Employer's obligations in the Construction Stage
10. D&M Contractor's obligations in the Construction Stage
11. Design
12. Employment of Trade Contractors
13. Administration of Trade Contractors and Sub-Consultants
14. D&M Contractor's liability regarding Trade Contractors and

Sub-Consultants
15. Works by persons other than the D&M Contractor, Trade Contractors or Sub-Consultants
16. Materials, goods and workmanship
17. Contingency, variations and additional works
18. Access
19. Commencement and completion
20. Readiness for Fitting Out, occupation, Practical Completion and defects liability
21. Extensions of time and delay
22. Injury to persons and property – insurance and indemnity
23. Insurance of the Works
24. D&M Contractor's, Trade Contractors' and Sub-Consultants' insurances
25. Regarding insurance generally
26. Determination by the Employer
27. Determination by the D&M Contractor
28. Payment
29. Adjustment of Target Cost
30. Statutory Tax Deduction Scheme
31. VAT – supplemental provisions
32. Set-off
33. Copyright and confidentiality
34. Objects of interest or value
35. Assignment and sub-letting
36. Settlement of disputes
37. Governing law

SCHEDULES
1   Employer's Representative, Architect, Structural Engineer, M&E Consultant, D&M Contractor's Project Manager, D&M Contractor's supporting staff, Defects Liability Period, liquidated and ascertained damages, insurances, retention percentage, VAT, Agreement, Adjudicator
2   Construction Stage Fee
3   D&M Contractor's services
4   Prime Cost
    Part A – Included Items (including Design Fee)
    Part B – Excluded Items
    Part C – D&M Contractor's staff – Schedule of Rates
    [Part D – Summary of Project Overheads]
5   Supplemental provisions – the VAT Agreement

ANNEXES
A   Form of parent company guarantee
B   Form of warranty agreement – Trade Contractors to Employer (Employer/Sub-Contractor Agreement)
C   Form of warranty agreement – Trade Contractors to third parties
D   Form of warranty agreement – Sub-Consultants to Employer
E   Form of warranty agreement – Sub-Consultants to third parties
F   Form of warranty agreement – D&M Contractor to third parties

G   Form of certificate for payment
H   Form of certificate of title
I   Form of appointment of Adjudicator

APPENDICES
A   The Brief
B   Part 1 – Employer's Requirements
     Part 2 – Construction Programme
     Part 3 – Target Cost
C   Form of Trade Contract
D   Form of Architect's Sub-Agreement
E   Form of Structural Engineer's Sub-Agreement
F   Form of M&E Consultant's Sub-Agreement
G   Project insurance

[A copy of the full contract is available upon application to Trench Farrow and Partners, 32 Chapter St, Westminster, London SW1 Telephone 071-931 7688.

Appendix 3: Explanatory memorandum summarising the proposed pro forma trade contract

This Explanatory Memorandum is not a Contract Document and is written to provide guidance only to the proposed full Contract documentation. Accordingly, while this Explanatory Memorandum is believed to be an accurate summary of the terms of the proposed pro forma Trade Contract, no responsibility can be accepted for any omissions or inaccuracies.

For convenience of use, copies of the Contents pages from the proposed pro forma Trade Contract are attached at the end of this Explanatory Memorandum.

Parties – (1) [. . . . .] Ltd ("the Employer") or (1) the Design and Management Contractor ("the D&M Contractor") and (2) the Trade Contractor ("the Trade Contractor"). The pro forma allows for two alternative situations: Alternative I where the Trade Contractor is employed initially by the Employer (i.e. a Pre-Ordered Trade Contract Package) and Alternative II where the Trade Contractor is employed initially by the D&M Contractor.

RECITALS
ALTERNATIVE I (Recitals (A) to (E))

(A) – Definitions of the Trade Contract Works and the Site. The definition of Trade Contract Works includes any preliminary design or other work previously carried out for the Employer, any necessary design or further design and any materials supplied by the Employer.

(B) – Definitions of the Project, the D&M Contract and the D&M Contractor. This Recital is in two alternatives, the first of which assumes that the D&M Contract will not yet have been entered into. The Trade Contractor acknowledges that it has had a reasonable opportunity of inspecting the D&M Contract.

(C) – The Project is presently in its Pre-Construction Stage. The Employer has the option not to proceed with the employment of the D&M Contractor for the Construction Stage.

(D) – The Trade Contractor is willing for this Trade Contract to be novated to the D&M Contractor (or an alternative design and management contractor) for the Construction Stage or, if the Employer opts to execute the Project in whole or in part itself, to proceed as if the Employer were the D&M Contractor. If the Employer opts not to proceed with the Project at all it shall be entitled to determine the Trade Contractor's employment under Clause 27.

(E) – Brief details of the Project together with drawings, specifications, etc.

describing the Trade Contract Works ("*the Tender Documents*") are listed in Appendix B. The Trade Contractor acknowledges that these may be subject to further detailed design by the Sub-Consultants.

ALTERNATIVE II (Recitals (A) to (D))

(A) – Definitions of the Trade Contract Works and the Site. The definition of Trade Contract Works includes any preliminary design or other work previously carried out for the Employer or the D&M Contractor, any necessary design or further design and any materials supplied by the Employer and/or the D&M Contractor.

(B) – Definitions of the Project, the D&M Contract and the Employer. The Trade Contractor acknowledges that it has had a reasonable opportunity of inspecting the D&M Contract.

(C) – The Project is now in its Construction Stage, and the D&M Contract accordingly includes the agreed Employer's Requirements, Construction Programme and Target Cost.

(D) – Brief details of the Project together with drawings, specifications, etc. describing the Trade Contract Works (*"the Tender Documents"*) are listed in Appendix B The Trade Contractor acknowledges that these may be subject to further detailed design by the Sub-Consultants.

ALTERNATIVES I AND II

(F)/(E) – Statements of whether the Trade Contractor, the D&M Contractor and the Employer are or are not "contractors" for the purposes of the Statutory Tax Deduction Scheme.

1. DEFINITIONS AND INTERPRETATION

1.1 Definitions.

1.2 Clause numbers, etc. relate to this Trade Contract unless otherwise stated.

1.3 Statutory references include amended, re-enacted or subordinate legislation.

1.4 Headings shall not affect the construction or interpretation of this Trade Contract.

1.5 The singular shall include the plural, etc.

1.6 Nothing in the Tender Documents shall override, modify or affect anything in any other of the Trade Contract Documents. Otherwise the Trade Contract Documents shall be mutually explanatory, but in the event of conflict these Conditions shall take precedence.

1.7 No consent or approval by the D&M Contractor, the Employer or any other person shall relieve the Trade Contractor of any of its liabilities or obligations under this Trade Contract.

2. SCOPE OF TRADE CONTRACT, NOVATION AND WARRANTY AGREEMENTS

ALTERNATIVE I (Clauses 2.1 to 2.9)

2.1 The Trade Contractor shall carry out and complete the Trade Contract Works (including any further design work) for the Trade Contract Sum in accordance with the provisions of this Trade Contract and in conformity with all instructions and further detailed designs issued to it.

2.2 The Trade Contract Sum shall be paid at the times and in the manner specified in this Trade Contract.

2.3 If the Employer proceeds with the D&M Contractor for the Construction Stage and the D&M Contractor supplies to the Trade Contractor copies of the Employer's Requirements, the Construction Programme and the Target Cost, then this Trade Contract shall be deemed to be novated to the D&M Contractor and the parties shall enter into a formal Novation Agreement in the form set out in *Schedule 1*. The Trade Contractor shall then be bound by and shall perform this Trade Contract in all respects as if the D&M Contractor had originally been a party to it in place of the Employer and shall release and discharge the Employer accordingly.

2.4 The expression *"[Employer/D&M Contractor]"* shall mean the Employer before any such novation and thereafter the D&M Contractor.

2.5 If the Employer opts not to proceed with the D&M Contractor or to terminate the D&M Contractor's employment for any other reason or to proceed with another design and management contractor or to execute the Project in whole or in part itself, then the Trade Contractor shall do everything reasonably required by the Employer to give effect thereto, including if appropriate by entering into a Novation Agreement in the form set out in *Schedule 1*. No person susequently appointed to perform the functions of the D&M Contractor shall be entitled to disregard or overrule any previous certificate, decision or instruction of the D&M Contractor.

2.6 The Trade Contractor shall provide a guarantee from its ultimate parent company in the form set out in *Schedule 2* and/or a performance bond in the form set out in *Schedule 3* within seven days of the execution of this Trade Contract. The Employer shall have no liability to the Trade Contractor unless and until these are provided.

2.7 A new or revised parent company guarantee and/or performance bond shall be provided within 14 days of any novation, and the D&M Contractor shall have no liability to the Trade Contractor unless and until these are provided.

2.8 Within 14 days after any novation the Trade Contractor shall enter into a Warranty Agreement under seal with the Employer in the form set out in *Schedule 4* and the D&M Contractor shall have no liability to the Trade Contractor unless and until this is provided.

2.9 The Trade Contractor undertakes to provide further Warranty Agreements in the form set out in *Schedule 5* in favour of any company or institution providing finance for the Trade Contract Works or any part thereof or of any purchaser or mortgagee of the Site or the completed Project or any part thereof or any or all of the Tenants as required by *Clause 4.1* of the *D&M Contract*, and the [Employer/D&M Contractor] shall have no liability or further liability to the Trade Contractor unless and until these are provided.

ALTERNATIVE II (Clauses 2.1 to 2.7)
2.1 The Trade Contractor shall carry out and complete the Trade Contract Works (including any further design work) for the Trade Contract Sum in accordance with the provisions of this Trade Contract and in conformity with all instructions and further detailed designs issued to it.

2.2 The Trade Contract Sum shall be paid at the times and in the manner specified in this Trade Contract.

2.3 The expression "[Employer/D&M Contractor]" shall be treated as referring solely to the D&M Contractor.

2.4 If the D&M Contractor's employment is terminated for any reason and the Employer opts to proceed with another design and management contractor or to execute the Project in whole or in part itself, then the Trade Contractor shall do everything reasonably required by the Employer to give effect thereto, including if appropriate by entering into a Novation Agreement in the form set out in *Schedule 1*. No person subsequently appointed to perform the functions of the D&M Contractor shall be entitled to disregard or overrule any previous certificate, decision or instruction of the D&M Contractor.

2.5 The Trade Contractor shall provide a guarantee from its ultimate parent company in the form set out in *Schedule 2* and/or a performance bond in the form set out in *Schedule 3* within seven days of the execution of this Trade Contract. The D&M Contractor shall have no liability to the Trade Contractor unless and until these are provided.

2.6 Within seven days of the execution of this Trade Contract the Trade Contractor shall enter into a Warranty Agreement under seal with the Employer in the form set out in *Schedule 4* and the D&M Contractor shall have no liability to the Trade Contractor unless and until this is provided.

2.7 The Trade Contractor undertakes to provide further Warranty Agreements in the form set out in *Schedule 5* in favour of any company or institution providing finance for the Trade Contract Works or of any purchaser or mortgagee of the Site or the completed Project or any part thereof or any or all of the Tenants as required by *Clause 4.1* of the *D&M Contract*, and the D&M Contractor shall have no liability or further liability to the Trade Contractor unless and until these are provided.

3. APPLICATION OF THE D&M CONTRACT
3.1 The Trade Contractor shall observe, perform and comply with all relevant provisions of the *D&M Contract* and shall carry out the Trade Contract Works so as not to constitute, cause or contribute to any breach thereof. Unless expressly otherwise provided, the Trade Contractor shall assume and perform all the obligations of the D&M Contractor under the *D&M Contract* insofar as they relate to the Trade Contract Works and shall indemnify the [Employer/D&M Contractor] against any liability thereunder arising from any negligence, default or breach of contract by the

Trade Contractor or its employees, agents or sub-contractors.

3.2 The Trade Contractor acknowledges that breaches of the Trade Contract may result in liability arising under the *D&M Contract* and otherwise and that it shall be fully liable to the D&M Contractor in respect of any such breaches, including for any resulting liability to the Employer.

3.3 The Trade Contractor shall not contend in any legal proceedings or otherwise that the effect of *Clause 14* of the *D&M Contract* (which limits the D&M Contractor's liability to the Employer to such sums as the D&M Contractor is able to recover from defaulting Trade Contractors or Sub-Consultants) is that the D&M Contractor has suffered no loss or that the Trade Contractor's liability to the D&M Contractor is thereby in any way reduced or extinguished.

4. TRADE CONTRACTOR'S OBLIGATIONS
4.1 This Trade Contract document and the Tender Documents together constitute the *Trade Contract Documents*.

4.2 The Trade Contractor shall carry out and complete the Trade Contract Works in all respects in accordance with the Trade Contract Documents and all reasonable directions of the [Employer/D&M Contractor].

4.3 The Trade Contractor shall be deemed to have full knowledge of and to have allowed for everything necessary to carry out and complete the Trade Contract Works and shall accordingly be deemed to have investigated and satisfied itself as to relevant Site conditions and facilities so far as reasonably possible. The Trade Contractor shall upon request provide the [Employer/D&M Contractor] with all such information in regard to the Trade Contract Works as it may reasonably require.

4.4 The Trade Contractor shall exercise all the skill, care and diligence to be expected of a suitably qualified and experienced contractor in the execution and completion of the Trade Contract Works.

4.5 The Trade Contractor shall notify the [Employer/D&M Contractor] of any ambiguities or discrepancies in the Trade Contract Documents or any further documents or instructions issued to it, and the [Employer/D&M Contractor] shall issue instructions accordingly. Where appropriate such instructions may be treated as variations under *Clause 13.1*.

5. INSTRUCTIONS AND DRAWINGS
5.1 The Trade Contractor shall forthwith comply with all instructions and directions unless it makes reasonable objection thereto within seven days. If the Trade Contractor fails to comply the [Employer/D&M Contractor] may employ others to execute the work at the Trade Contractor's cost.

5.2 All instructions shall be in writing.

5.3 The Trade Contractor may apply to the [Employer/D&M Contractor] for further drawings, details or specifications reasonably necessary to enable it to carry out the Trade Contract Works. The [Employer/D&M Contractor] shall provide without charge three copies of any such drawings and details (and a further two copies of any amended or revised drawings) and one copy of any such specifications. The provision of these further design details shall not constitute a variation under *Clause 13.1* unless the [Employer/D&M Contractor] so instructs, and if the Trade Contractor considers that any do constitute a variation it must advise the [Employer/D&M Contractor] within 14 days.

6. STATUTORY REQUIREMENTS

6.1 The Trade Contractor shall comply with all Statutory Requirements and shall give all necessary notices where this is required by the Trade Contract Documents.

6.2 The Trade Contractor shall check for conflicts with the Statutory Requirements and immediately notify the [Employer/D&M Contractor] of any it may find, together with its proposals for overcoming the same. The [Employer/D&M Contractor] shall then issue appropriate instructions, which may constitute variations under *Clause 13.1* (although changes in the design or selection of components shall be deemed to have been allowed for by the Trade Contractor).

6.3 The Trade Contractor shall pay and indemnify the [Employer/D&M Contractor] against all fees and charges payable under the Statutory Requirements. These shall be added to the Trade Contract Sum unless they are stated to be included in it.

6.4 The Trade Contractor shall immediately supply to the [Employer/D&M Contractor] copies of all notices, etc. given or received.

7. OTHER PROJECT WORKS

7.1 The Trade Contractor shall satisfy itself in adequate time as to the position, dimensions and suitability of any work carried out by others and shall immediately advise the [Employer/D&M Contractor] if such work is in any way unsuitable so as to enable (where practicable) rectification work to be undertaken before the scheduled commencement of the Trade Contract Works.

7.2 The Trade Contractor shall have no claim against the Employer or the D&M Contractor in respect of any such unsuitable work carried out by others unless it has given such timely notice and the unsuitability materially affects the Trade Contract Works.

7.3 Unless the [Employer/D&M Contractor] otherwise instructs, the Trade Contractor shall be entirely responsible for the consequences of its own inaccurate setting out.

7.4 The Trade Contractor shall permit contemporaneous work by others as envisaged in *Clauses 15 and 20.1* of the *D&M Contract* and shall comply with any *Access Regime Documents* and all reasonable directions.

8. MATERIALS, GOODS AND WORKMANSHIP

8.1 Materials, goods and workmanship shall comply with all relevant specifications and instructions. If any specified materials, goods or workmanship are not procurable the Trade Contractor shall propose suitable alternatives and obtain the [Employer/D&M Contractor's] consent thereto. Such consent shall not relieve the Trade Contractor of any of his obligations, and any alternatives agreed shall not affect the Trade

Contract Sum unless the [Employer/D&M Contractor] notifies the Trade Contractor that the substitution constitutes a variation under *Clause 13.1*.

8.2 The Trade Contractor shall upon request furnish the [Employer/D&M Contractor] with all test certificates, etc., retain all relevant vouchers and certificates and procure that the benefit of any manufacturer's or supplier's warranties is passed on to the Employer.

8.3 The Trade Contractor shall be fully responsible for the compliance of all materials and goods used in or for the Trade Contract Works and shall carry out all necessary inspections to satisfy itself as to the standard and condition of any materials or goods supplied by others (including the D&M Contractor and/or the Employer).

8.4 The [Employer/D&M Contractor] may require the opening up of work for inspection or for the carrying out of additional tests. The cost thereof shall be added to the Trade Contract Sum unless the relevant work, materials or goods are not in accordance with this Trade Contract. If at any time any non-compliance with this Trade Contract is discovered the Trade Contractor shall immediately advise the [Employer/D&M Contractor] as to the action it proposes to take to establish that there is no similar failure in work already executed or materials or goods already supplied, and if satisfactory proposals are not received within five days the [Employer/D&M Contractor] may require opening up or additional tests to establish that no similar failure has occurred elsewhere.

8.5 The [Employer/D&M Contractor] may require the removal and re-execution or repair of any work not in accordance with the Trade Contract.

9. INTELLECTUAL PROPERTY RIGHTS
9.1 All royalties, etc. are deemed to be included in the Trade Contract Sum. The Trade Contractor shall indemnify the Employer and the D&M Contractor against any claims for infringement of any patent or other intellectual property rights.

9.2 Copyright in all documents and materials will be retained by the Trade Contractor, but the [Employer/D&M Contractor] shall be granted a royalty-free, irrevocable and non-exclusive licence to use and reproduce such documents and materials for all purposes relating to the Project.

10. TRADE CONTRACTOR'S SUPERVISOR
10.1 The Trade Contact Works shall be supervised by a supervisor and supervision team previously approved by the [Employer/D&M Contractor], which shall not be changed without the [Employer/D&M Contractor]'s consent.

10.2 The [Employer/D&M Contractor] may at any time reasonably require the removal of any person employed on the Site.

11. ACCESS FOR THE D&M CONTRACTOR, THE EMPLOYER, ETC.
The D&M Contractor, the Employer and all persons authorised by them shall at all reasonable times have access to any place where work is being prepared or stored for the Trade Contract Works.

12. TRADE CONTRACTOR'S DESIGN

12.1 Where the Trade Contract Works contain a design element the Trade Contractor shall carry out and complete such design and shall comply with any directions which the [Employer/D&M Contractor] or any Sub-Consultant may give for the co-ordination or integration of such design with the design of the Project. The Trade Contractor shall be responsible for the design of all its temporary works, which shall take into account subterranean conditions, the requirements of adjoining properties and the possible use thereof by others. The Trade Contractor acknowledges that the D&M Contractor and the Employer will be relying on its skill and judgement.

12.2 In relation to the Trade Contractor's design obligations:

12.2.1 The Trade Contractor warrants that it will exercise all the skill, care and diligence to be expected of a suitably qualified and experienced contractor.

12.2.2 The Trade Contractor warrants that its design and all materials and goods used therein will satisfy any applicable performance specification or requirement and comply with the Statutory Requirements and the Employer's Requirements, that such materials and goods will be and remain of merchantable quality and fit for their required purposes and that no deleterious materials or goods will be recommended or selected by the Trade Contractor or incorporated into the Trade Contract Works.

12.2.3 The Trade Contractor shall without charge provide the [Employer/D&M Contractor] with the specified number of copies of all its design documents in a timely manner. No such documents shall be used for fabrication or construction until authorised by the [Employer/D&M Contractor], but no such authorisation shall relieve the Trade Contractor of any responsibility or liability.

12.2.4 Payments for work executed or materials or goods supplied in connection with the Trade Contractor's design shall be conditional upon the Trade Contractor's compliance with such authorisation procedures.

12.3 The Trade Contractor shall not be entitled to any extension of time or reimbursement of loss and expense or to terminate its employment where and to the extent that the cause of the relevant delay, matter or event is an error, omission, etc. in the Trade Contractor's design or a failure by the Trade Contractor to provide design documents in a timely manner or a divergence from the Statutory Requirements (other than where the result of legislative changes after the execution of the Trade Contract).

12.4 Errors, omissions, etc. in the Trade Contractor's design shall be corrected at its own cost and with no extension of time. The Trade Contractor shall indemnify the Employer and the D&M Contractor in respect of any such errors, omissions, etc.

12.5 At or before Practical Completion of each Section the Trade Contractor shall provide six copies of as built drawings and draft service manuals, and Practical Completion shall not take place until these are provided.

12.6 Within three months after Practical Completion of the final Section the

Trade Contractor shall provide six copies of all drawings, specifications and other details relating to any works constructed in accordance with the Trade Contractor's design as built, together with service manuals.

13. VARIATIONS AND PROVISIONAL SUMS

13.1 The [Employer/D&M Contractor] may issue instructions requiring variations. All instructions requiring variations shall be in writing and shall expressly state that they are intended as such.

13.2 The term "variation" includes any addition, omission, substitution, alteration or modification of any performance requirement or of any element of the Trade Contract Works, including the addition of fitting-out works.

13.3 The [Employer/D&M Contractor] may issue instructions in regard to the expenditure of provisional sums.

13.4 The [Employer/D&M Contractor] may require the Trade Contractor to submit assessments of the cost and time implication of proposed variations. If the parties, in consultation with the Employer's Representative, are able to agree any such assessment it shall become binding upon the Trade Contractor. If agreement cannot be reached the [Employer/D&M Contractor] may nevertheless require the Trade Contractor to proceed or may withdraw the proposed variation. The [Employer/D&M Contractor] may also dispense with this procedure at any time.

13.5 Subject to *Clause 13.4*, all variations and provisional sum work shall be measured and valued by the [Employer/D&M Contractor], after consulting with the Trade Contractor, in accordance with *Clauses 13.5.1 to 13.5.7*, as follows:

13.5.1 Where work is of a similar character and there is no significant change in quantities the prices in the contract bills, etc. shall apply. Where work is of a similar character but conditions are dissimilar or there is a significant change in quantities such prices shall apply but with a fair allowance for such difference in conditions and/or quantities.

13.5.2 Work which is not of a similar character shall be priced on the basis of a fair valuation.

13.5.3 Where the [Employer/D&M Contractor] agrees in advance, daywork may be allowed at the rates stated in the Tender Documents or, if none, at the prime cost thereof plus the percentage additions stated in the Tender Documents. Daily vouchers will be required.

13.5.4 Omissions shall be valued in accordance with *Clause 13.5.1*, with any work substantially affected thereby valued in accordance with *Clause 13.5.2*.

13.5.5 The Trade Contractor shall have the opportunity of being present at any measurement of work.

13.5.6 The Trade Contractor shall provide the [Employer/D&M Contractor] with all reasonable additional facilities required for any measurement and valuation.

13.5.7 The cost of work necessitated by any negligence, default or breach of contract by the Trade Contractor or its employees, agents or sub-contractors shall not be included, and nor shall any allowance for delay or direct loss and/or expense for which the Trade Contractor would be reimbursed under any other provision.

13.6 Price changes arising from variations and provisional sum work shall be taken into account in interim payments nd by adjustment of the Trade Contract Sum.

13.7 The Trade Contractor may make direct loss and/or expense claims arising from variations or provisional sum work within 30 days of the loss or expense being incurred. The amount of any such loss or expense shall be ascertained by the [Employer/D&M Contractor], added to the Trade Contract Sum and paid with the next interim payment.

13.8 The [Employer/D&M Contractor] may instruct the Trade Contractor to carry out fitting-out works as envisaged in *Clause 17.5* of the *D&M Contract* as a variation and as a separate Section of the Trade Contract Works and may issue further instructions or directions in relation thereto.

14. TRADE CONTRACT SUM
14.1 The Trade Contract Sum shall only be adjusted in accordance with the express provisions of this Trade Contract and, subject to *Clause 14.3*, errors in computation are deemed to have been accepted.

14.2 Errors in description or quantity or by omission of items from the Tender Documents shall be corrected and deemed to be variations, but without cost or time implications.

14.3 The design and manufacture element and the delivery and installation element of the Trade Contract Sum are separately identified in *Appendix C*. The design and manufacture element has an all-inclusive fixed lump sum price, save for variations and provisional sum work. The delivery and installation element may either have a fixed lump sum price or be subject to fluctuations in accordance with the formula and conditions set out in *Appendix C* or be partly one and partly the other. All valuations of variations and provisional sum work shall separately identify the two elements.

14.4 The Trade Contract Sum shall be deemed to include all costs, charges, expenses, overheads and profit.

15. VALUE ADDED TAX
15.1 References to "tax" mean VAT.

15.2 The Trade Contact Sum is exclusive of VAT, which shall be chargeable in accordance with applicable legislation and with the VAT Agreement (which follows the usual JCT form, except that payments will only be made by the [Employer/D&M Contractor] against VAT invoices rather than authenticated receipts).

16. UNFIXED MATERIALS AND GOODS – RISK
16.1 The [Employer/D&M Contractor] may at any time instruct the Trade Contractor to deliver materials or goods to the Site.

16.2 Unfixed materials and goods shall not be removed from the Site without the [Employer/D&M Contractor]'s consent, which shall not be unreasonably withheld. Materials and goods shall become the property of the Employer upon delivery to the Site.

16.3 Off-Site materials and goods included in any interim payment shall become the property of the Employer, and the Trade Contractor shall then move them from where they are only for use upon the Trade Contract Works. The Trade Contractor shall nevertheless be responsible for loss or damage and for the cost of storage and handling.

16.4 Risk of loss or damage to the Trade Contract Works shall remain with the Trade Contractor until Practical Completion of the relevant Section. The Trade Contractor shall at its own cost protect the Trade Contract Works, including any particular protection required by the Trade Contract Documents or as directed by the [Employer/D&M Contractor].

16.5 The Trade Contractor shall at its own cost make good any loss or damage to the Trade Contract Works occurring before Practical Completion and shall comply with any instructions issued by the [Employer/D&M Contractor] to that effect.

16.6 Where loss or damage is caused by the negligence, default or breach of contract of any other trade contractor the [Employer/D&M Contractor] shall seek to recover the costs of making good on the Trade Contractor's behalf and shall pay any amount recovered (after deduction of legal and other costs) to the Trade Contractor.

17. PRACTICAL COMPLETION AND DEFECTS LIABILITY

17.1 The stated Defects Liability Period for each section shall commence from the date of Practical Completion. The [Employer/D&M Contractor] may extend the Defects Liability Period in respect of any Section so as to continue until the expiry of the relevant Defects Liability Period under the D&M Contract, in which event there shall be added to the Trade Contract Sum the additional fixed amount stated in or calculated in accordance with *Appendix A*.

17.2 The [Employer/D&M Contractor] shall issue certificates of Practical Completion for each Section. The [Employer/D&M Contractor] may issue a snagging list before, at or after Practical Completion, and the Trade Contractor shall forthwith make good such snagging items. Upon Practical Completion the Trade Contractor shall leave each Section clean and tidy to the reasonable satisfaction of the [Employer/D&M Contractor].

17.3 The [Employer/D&M Contractor] shall deliver a schedule of defects to the Trade Contractor within 14 days after the expiry of the Defects Liability Period. The Trade Contractor shall make good such defects within 14 days of receipt thereof, unless the [Employer/D&M Contractor] otherwise instructs (in which event an appropriate deduction shall be made).

17.4 The [Employer/D&M Contractor] may issue instructions requiring the making good of defects at any time during the Defects Liability Period.

17.5 The [Employer/D&M Contractor] shall issue a Certificate of Making

Good Defects when all incomplete items and defects have been completed and made good.

17.6 Such work of making good shall be carried out in accordance with a programme to be specified by the [Employer/D&M Contractor], which may require work wholly or partly outside normal working hours (with any additional costs being the responsibility of the Trade Contractor).

18. ASSIGNMENT AND SUB-LETTING

18.1 The Trade Contractor shall not assign or sub-let without the [Employer/D&M Contractor]'s consent. Subject to *Clause 25.3.3*, any sub-letting must determine on the determination of the Trade Contractor's employment.

18.2 No sub-letting or consent to sub-letting shall relieve the Trade Contractor of any of its responsibilities or obligations.

19. INDEMNITY BY THE TRADE CONTRACTOR

19.1 The Trade Contractor shall indemnify the Employer and the D&M Contractor against third party personal injury and damage to property claims, except to the extent due to any act or neglect of the Employer or the D&M Contractor or their representatives.

19.2 Such indemnity and the Trade Contractor's insurance obligations under *Clause 20* shall not extend to damage, loss or injury caused by radiation, nuclear risks or pressure waves.

19.3 If the [Employer/D&M Contractor] shall make good any defects for which the Trade Contractor is responsible the Trade Contractor shall pay or allow to the [Employer/D&M Contractor] the cost thereof and shall indemnify the [Employer/D&M Contractor] in respect thereof.

19.4 Without prejudice to its other rights or remedies or to the final determination of the amount of any liability, the Trade Contractor shall forthwith pay or allow to the [Employer/D&M Contractor], or the [Employer/D&M Contractor] may deduct from subsequent interim payments, the [Employer/D&M Contractor]'s good faith estimate of any damage, cost, loss and/or expense caused or likely to be caused to the [Employer/D&M Contractor] by any breach of this Trade Contract or any negligence, default or breach of contract for which the Trade Contractor is responsible.

19.5 The amount of any such damage, cost, loss and/or expense shall be ascertained by the [Employer/D&M Contractor] and deducted from the Trade Contract Sum and from subsequent interim payments. If any estimated amount has already been deducted the difference shall be payable to the [Employer/D&M Contractor] or to the Trade Contractor, as the case may be.

19.6 The Trade Contractor shall at all times prevent any public or private nuisance or other interference with the rights of any adjoining or neighbouring landowner, tenant or occupier or any statutory undertaker and shall assist the Employer in defending any relevant proceedings. The Trade Contractor shall indemnify the Employer and the D&M Contractor in respect thereof, save only where such nuisance or interference results from any variation or other instruction of the [Employer/D&M Contractor] (unless itself caused by the Trade Contractor) and which could not reasonably have been avoided by the Trade Contractor.

19.7 The Trade Contractor shall ensure that there is no trespass on or over any adjoining or neighbouring property and shall obtain all necessary agreements with adjoining owners, included crane licences, on terms previously approved by the [Employer/D&M Contractor].

20. TRADE CONTRACTOR'S INSURANCES

20.1 The Trade Contractor shall maintain all such insurances as are necessary to cover the liabilities referred to in *Clause 19*, including employer's liability insurance, for at least the minimum cover shown in *Appendix A* and with the Employer and the D&M Contractor indemnified as joint insureds.

20.2 Such insurances shall be effected with insurers previously approved by the [Employer/D&M Contractor].

20.3 The Trade Contractor shall produce evidence of such insurances and receipts therefore when required by the Employer's Representative or the [Employer/D&M Contractor].

20.4 If the Trade Contractor fails to insure the [Employer/D&M Contractor] may itself do so and recover the premium from the Trade Contractor.

21. PROJECT INSURANCES

21.1 The D&M Contractor shall ensure that the Project and other insurances required under *Clauses 23 and 24* of the *D&M Contract* are in place before the Trade Contractor commences work and that such insurances either include the Trade Contractor as an insured or waive any right of subrogation up to the date of Practical Completion. The Trade Contractor need not maintain any separate insurance of the Trade Contract Works unless so required pursuant to *Clause 24.2* of the *D&M Contract*.

21.2 The Trade Contractor shall strictly observe and comply with the conditions of such insurance policies.

21.3 The [Employer/D&M Contractor] shall not be obliged to insure the Trade Contractor's temporary buildings, plant, tools and equipment.

21.4 *Clause 25* of the *D&M Contract* shall apply on a back-to-back basis in relation to the restoration of any damage to the Trade Contract Works.

22. COMMENCEMENT AND COMPLETION

22.1 The Trade Contract Works shall be commenced on the date stated in the Trade Contract Programme (or otherwise in accordance with the [Employer/D&M Contractor]'s instruction to proceed) and shall then be regularly and diligently carried out so as to ensure completion of each Section in accordance with the Trade Contract Programme.

22.2 The [Employer/D&M Contractor] will give the Trade Contractor access (or further access) to so much of the Site as may be required. The Trade Contractor shall not have exclusive or uninterrupted access to any part of the Site and shall make due allowance for and not unreasonably impede other trade contractors or other persons employed on the Site. The [Employer/D&M Contractor] does not warrant continuity of working. The [Employer/D&M Contractor] may issue directions to co-ordinate the execution of the Trade Contract Works with other work on the Site, including by alteration of the sequence of the Trade Contract Works, and no extension of time or adjustment to the Trade Contract Sum shall be made in consequence thereof.

22.3 Without prejudice to *Clause 19.4* or to the final ascertainment of the amount of any liability, the Trade Contractor shall forthwith pay or allow to the [Employer/D&M Contractor], or the [Employer/D&M Contractor] may deduct from subsequent interim payments, the [Employer/D&M Contractor]'s good faith estimate of any loss or damage suffered or likely to be suffered by the [Employer/D&M Contractor] in consequence of the breach which the Employer's Representative reasonably considers there to have been by the Trade Contractor of any of its obligations under *Clause 22.1*.

22.4 The [Employer/D&M Contractor] may postpone the Trade Contract Works in whole or in part and reimburse the Trade Contractor its resulting direct loss and/or expense.

23. EXTENSION OF TIME

23.1 The Trade Contractor shall forthwith notify the [Employer/D&M Contractor] (and update it as necessary) as to the cause and implications of any delay or likely delay in the progress of the Trade Contract Works.

23.2 Provided the Trade Contractor has complied with *Clause 23.1*, the [Employer/D&M Contractor] shall grant fair and reasonable extensions of time to reflect delays to the completion of any Section caused by any of the matters or events listed in *Clauses 23.2.1* to *23.2.8* (but subject always to *Clauses 23.2.9* to *23.2.12*) as follows:

23.2.1 Events which are neither within the control of, nor reasonably foreseeable by, the Trade Contractor (but excluding unavailability of labour, goods or materials);

23.2.2 Loss or damage caused by fire, etc.;

23.2.3 Instructions issued by the [Employer/D&M Contractor] under *Clause 13.1, 13.3 or 22.4*;

23.2.4 Late receipt of instructions, drawings, etc.;

23.2.5 Any breach or act of prevention by the [Employer/D&M Contractor] or its representatives, including failure to provide access or essential facilities;

23.2.6 Opening up, testing and making good (unless the work, materials or goods are defective);

23.2.7 Execution of work by others or any failure to execute such work (unless such possibility was allowed for or reasonably foreseeable by the Trade Contractor);

23.2.8 Work by local authorities or statutory undertakers or failure to carry out such work.

23.2.9 The Trade Contractor shall use constantly its best endeavours to prevent or minimise delay.

23.2.10 The [Employer/D&M Contractor] may take into account the effects of omissions when determining any extension of time.

23.2.11 The Trade Contractor shall not be entitled to any extension of time if the delay was provided for in the Trade Contract Documents or caused by circumstances which the Trade Contractor was required to take into account or caused by any negligence, default or breach of contract of the Trade Contractor or its representatives.

23.2.12 The [Employer/D&M Contractor] may at any time up to 12 weeks after Practical Completion review any previous extension of time granted, but so that no period for completion shall be made shorter than as stated in the original Trade Contract Programme unless work has been omitted.

23.3 Where an extension of time has been agreed under *Clause 13.4.2* no further or other extension shall be granted.

23.4 Within 14 days of any extension of time the Trade Contractor shall submit a revised programme for the [Employer/D&M Contractor]'s approval, which when approved shall become the new Trade Contract Programme.

24. LOSS AND EXPENSE
24.1 The Trade Contractor shall be entitled to reimbursement of direct loss and/or expense arising from any of the matters or events listed in *Clauses 23.2.4 to 23.2.7* which materially affects the regular progress of the Trade Contract Works if within 30 days of such matter or event it submits an application to the [Employer/D&M Contractor] detailing the cause and implications thereof and subsequently provides such further details and reasonable assistance as the [Employer/D&M Contractor] may require. Any such amount shall be added to the Trade Contract Sum and to the next interim payment.

24.2 Subject to *Clause 24.3*, the provisions of *Clause 24.1* are without prejudice to the Trade Contractor's other rights and remedies.

24.3 Notwithstanding *Clauses 24.1* and *24.2*, the Trade Contractor shall not be entitled to recover any loss and/or expense resulting from strikes, etc. (as referred to in *Clause 33*).

25. DETERMINATION BY THE [EMPLOYER/D&M CONTRACTOR]
25.1 The [Employer/D&M Contractor] may determine the Trade Contractor's employment for default if the Trade Contractor continues such default for seven days after receipt of a default notice.

25.2 The [Employer/D&M Contractor] may forthwith determine the Trade Contractor's employment in the event of insolvency. The Trade Contractor shall immediately inform the [Employer/D&M Contractor] of any relevant proposals or petitions.

25.3 If the Trade Contractor's employment is determined for default or insolvency:

25.3.1 The [Employer/D&M Contractor] may employ others to complete the work using the Trade Contractor's temporary buildings, plant, tools, equipment, goods and materials;

25.3.2 The Trade Contractor shall properly furnish to the [Employer/D&M Contractor] two copies of all documents prepared or in the course of preparation;

25.3.3 If so required, the Trade Contractor shall assign to the [Employer/D&M Contractor] the benefit of all sub-contracts, in which event the [Employer/D&M Contractor] may make direct payments to the suppliers or sub-contractors and recover such payments from the Trade Contractor;

25.3.4 The Trade Contractor shall when so required (but not before) remove from the Site all temporary buildings, plant, tools, equipment, goods and materials, failing which the [Employer/D&M Contractor] may remove and sell the same and hold the proceeds (less costs) to the credit of the Trade Contractor;

25.3.5 The Trade Contractor shall allow or pay to the [Employer/D&M Contractor] any loss and/or damage caused to the [Employer/D&M Contractor] by the determination. The Employer shall not be bound to make any further payment to the Trade Contractor until after completion of the Project, whereupon the [Employer/D&M Contractor] shall certify the amount of the expenses properly incurred by the [Employer/D&M Contractor] in completing the work and the amount of such loss and/or damage. The appropriate net payment shall then be made to the [Employer/D&M Contractor] by the Trade Contractor or vice versa.

25.4 The [Employer/D&M Contractor] may forthwith determine the Trade Contractor's employment by notice at any time prior to the commencement by the Trade Contractor of work on Site. The Trade Contractor shall then be paid in full settlement (but without prejudice to any rights or remedies of the [Employer/D&M Contractor] in respect of prior breaches) a proportionate part of the Trade Contract Sum together with the cost of materials or goods properly ordered for which the Trade Contractor has paid or is legally bound to pay, which will then become the property of the Employer. The Trade Contractor shall promptly furnish to the [Employer/D&M Contractor] two copies of all preliminary drawings, etc., whether or not completed.

25.5 The [Employer/D&M Contractor] may forthwith determine the Trade Contractor's employment at any time without cause. The Trade Contractor shall then promptly furnish to the [Employer/D&M Contractor] two copies of all documents referred to in *Clause 25.3.2*, and the provisions of *Clause 26.2* shall apply.

26. DETERMINATION BY THE TRADE CONTRACTOR

26.1 The Trade Contractor may terminate its employment if the [Employer/D&M Contractor] fails to make any payment within 28 days of receipt of a default notice or if the Trade Contract Works are suspended for a continuous period of six months by reason of any instructions of the [Employer/D&M Contractor] (unless caused by any negligence, default or breach of contract of the Trade Contractor) or if the [Employer/D&M Contractor] becomes insolvent.

26.2 In such event:

26.2.1 The Trade Contractor shall remove from the Site all temporary buildings, plant, tools, equipment, goods and materials;

26.2.2 The Trade Contractor shall promptly furnish to the [Employer/D&M Contractor] two copies of all documents prepared or in the course of preparation;

26.2.3 The Trade Contractor shall be paid the total value of work completed, the total value of work begun but not completed (valued as if it were a variation), any direct loss and/or expense under *Clauses 13.7 and 24*, the cost of materials or goods properly ordered for which the Trade Contractor has paid or is legally bound to pay (such materials or goods then becoming the property of the Employer), its reasonable removal costs and any other direct loss and/or damage caused to the Trade Contractor by the determination.

26.2.4 Payment under *Clause 26.2.3* shall be in full settlement (but without prejudice to any rights or remedies of the [Employer/D&M Contractor] in respect of prior breaches).

27. DETERMINATION FOR NEUTRAL CAUSES OR ON TERMINATION OF THE D&M CONTRACT

27.1 Either party may determine if the Trade Contract Works are suspended for a continuous period of six months by force majeure, loss or damage caused by fire, etc. or riot or civil commotion, provided these are not caused by any negligence, default or breach of contract of the party serving the notice.

27.2 If the D&M Contractor's employment under the D&M Contract is determined for any reason the Employer shall be entitled in the name of the D&M Contractor to determine the Trade Contractor's employment.

27.3 Upon any determination under *Clause 27.1* or *27.2* the provisions of *Clause 26.2* (other than *Clause 26.2.3*) shall apply. In the case of a determination under *Clause 27.2* the provisions of *Clause 26.5* of the *D&M Contract* (regarding completion of the work by the Employer) shall also apply, and the Trade Contractor shall take all necessary steps to give effect thereto.

28. PUBLICITY

28.1 The Trade Contractor shall not issue any publicity materials without the Employer's Representative's consent.

28.2 The Trade Contractor shall not disclose any confidential information to any third party either during the continuance of this Trade Contract or afterwards.

28.3 The Trade Contract Documents and all other information supplied to the Trade Contractor shall not be used for any other purpose and shall be returned upon request at any time after Practical Completion of the final Section.

29. PAYMENT
ALTERNATIVE I

29.1 Prior to any novation of this Trade Contract the Trade Contractor shall submit monthly payment applications to the Employer's Representative together with such further documentation as he may reasonably require to verify such applications. The Employer's Representative shall verify or amend the amount applied for and issue an interim certificate for payment within 21 days, together if appropriate with a statement regarding any amounts disallowed. The value of materials and goods on Site will not be included if they are prematurely delivered or are not adequately stored and protected. The Employer shall pay the Trade Contractor the amount due within 14 days after the date of the interim certificate or within seven days of receipt of an appropriate VAT invoice, whichever is the later.

29.2 After any novation of this Trade Contract the D&M Contractor will provide such information to the Employer's Representative as will enable him to include in interim certificates issued under the *D&M Contract* the value of the Trade Contract Works then completed, and the Trade Contractor shall provide information to the D&M Contractor accordingly. Subject to receipt of an appropriate VAT invoice (if requested by the D&M Contractor), the D&M Contractor shall pay the Trade Contractor within 21 days of receipt of any such interim certificate the amount therein certified in respect of the Trade Contract Works.

ALTERNATIVE II

29.1 The D&M Contractor will provide such information to the Employer's Representative as will enable him to include in interim certificates issued under the *D&M Contract* the value of the Trade Contract Works then completed, and the Trade Contractor shall provide information to the D&M Contractor accordingly. The value of materials and goods on Site will not be included if they are prematurely delivered or are not adequately stored and protected.

29.2 Subject to receipt of an appropriate VAT invoice (if requested by the D&M Contractor), the D&M Contractor shall pay the Trade Contractor within 21 days of receipt of any such interim certificate the amount therein certified in respect of the Trade Contract Works.

ALTERNATIVES I AND II

29.3 The [Employer/D&M Contractor] may deduct retentions at the stated Retention Percentage from all interim payments prior to Practical Completion, and at the rate of half the Retention Percentage from any subsequent interim payments. The [Employer/D&M Contractor] shall hold such retentions on trust (but without obligation to invest). Half the retention applicable to any Section shall be released within 28 days after Practical Completion of that Section (or after completion of snagging items): the balance shall be released within 28 days after the expiry of the

Defects Liability Period (or after the Certificate of Completion of Making Good Defects).

29.4 Where the Employer's Representative has agreed to include off-Site materials or goods in interim certificates these shall be reflected in interim payments under the Trade Contract, provided the Trade Contractor shall observe any relevant conditions set out in the D&M Contract. The Trade Contractor shall in any event furnish certificates of title in respect thereof with such supporting evidence as the [Employer/D&M Contractor] may require.

29.5 The Trade Contractor shall co-operate fully in the verification of applications for payment by the Employer's Representative and shall provide such facilities and copy documents as the Employer's Representative is entitled to call for under the D&M Contract.

29.6 Not later than 30 days after Practical Completion of any Section the Trade Contractor shall send the [Employer/D&M Contractor] all further documents necessary for final measurement and valuation, which will be completed within three months after receipt thereof. The [Employer/D&M Contractor] may require such documents to be provided and final measurement and valuation to be carried out in respect of any part of the Trade Contract Works as soon as practicable (and in any event within 30 days) after it has been carried out. A final statement of account shall be provided to the Trade Contractor, who shall sign and return it to the [Employer/D&M Contractor] with seven days. Such signature shall be conclusive evidence that the amount shown is accepted in full and final settlement of all financial claims (other than for VAT).

29.7 In the settlement of accounts the Trade Contract Sum shall be adjusted to reflect actual expenditure of provisional sums.

29.8 The [Employer/D&M Contractor] may at its discretion release the final payment for any Section to the Trade Contractor at any time after Practical Completion thereof, subject to the Trade Contractor certifying that such payment is in full and final settlement and satisfying any further conditions which the [Employer/D&M Contractor] may require.

29.9 Not later than three months from completion of making good defects in respect of the final Section and receipt of the documents referred to in *Clause 29.6* the [Employer/D&M Contractor] shall issue the Final Certificate. The Final Certificate shall state the total already paid to the Trade Contractor, the adjusted Trade Contract Sum and the final balance due, which (subject to receipt of an appropriate VAT invoice) shall be payable 28 days thereafter.

29.10 Save in respect of fraud, the Final Certificate shall in any proceedings be conclusive evidence that materials and workmanship are where necessary to the reasonable satisfaction of the [Employer/D&M Contractor], that apart from errors or omissions the payment terms have been correctly implemented, that all appropriate extensions of time have been given and that any reimbursement to the Trade Contractor of direct loss and/or expense is in full and final settlement. The Final Certificate shall in no circumstances be conclusive as to the sufficiency of any design.

29.11 If proceedings have already been commenced the Final Certificate shall be conclusive as stated in *Clause 29.10* either after such proceedings have been concluded or after a period of 12 months inactivity in such proceedings, whichever is the earlier.

29.12 If proceedings are commenced within 28 days after the Final Certificate it shall be conclusive as stated in *Clause 29.10* save only in respect of matters to which those proceedings relate.

29.13 Save as provided in *Clauses 29.10, 29.11* and *29.12,* no certificate shall of itself be conclusive evidence that any materials, goods or work are in accordance with this Trade Contract.

29.14 Nothing in this Trade Contract shall limit or exclude the [Employer/D&M Contractor]'s rights of deduction or set-off.

30. STATUTORY TAX DEDUCTION SCHEME

30.1 to 30.9 These provisions relating to the operation of the Statutory Tax Deduction Scheme follow the usual JCT provisions.

31. ATTENDANCES AND SHARED FACILITIES

31.1 The Trade Contractor shall have free of charge the reasonable use in common with others of the attendances, facilities and services specified in the Tender Documents. Such use shall be at the sole risk of the Trade Contractor, who shall indemnify the D&M Contractor and the Employer against any claims and who shall make good at his own expense any damage, loss or injury. The [Employer/D&M Contractor] shall not be liable to the Trade Contactor for any failure in any way relating to the provision of such attendances, facilities or services except to the extent that the [Employer/D&M Contractor] can recover from the person responsible for the failure (unless an employee or agent of the [Employer/D&M Contractor]).

31.2 *Clause 31.1* shall not affect liability for death or personal injury.

32. CONDUCT ON SITE

32.1 The Trade Contractor shall strictly comply with any rules or regulations issued by the [Employer/D&M Contractor] governing the conduct of work on the Site.

32.2 Subject thereto, the Trade Contractor shall observe and provide everything necessary to comply with the relevant statutory provisions relating to work on the Site.

32.3 The Trade Contractor shall indemnify the Employer and the D&M Contractor for any breach of *Clauses 32.1* and *32.2.*

32.4 The Trade Contractor shall allow for the incomplete state of the Project and for adjacent work carried out by others. Safety devices provided by others shall not be relied upon. The Trade Contractor shall comply with the [Employer/D&M Contractor]'s requirements and directions on matters affecting the safe conduct of work on the Site.

32.5 The Trade Contractor shall take all necessary precautions to ensure the safety of and minimum inconvenience to the general public, Tenants and adjoining owners or occupiers.

32.6 The Trade Contractor shall provide the [Employer/D&M Contractor] with a copy of all its safety procedures, etc. and shall notify the [Employer/D&M Contractor] in advance of any dangerous or hazardous activity and of how it intends to carry out the same.

32.7 The Trade Contractor shall comply with any restrictions on working hours.

32.8 The Trade Contractor shall comply with Clause 34 of the D&M Contract with regard to objects of interest and value.

33. STRIKES
If the Project or the Trade Contract Works are affected by strikes, etc., then, without prejudice to any other rights or remedies under this Trade Contract:

33.1 Neither party shall be entitled to claim for any resulting loss and expense;

33.2 The [Employer/D&M Contractor] shall take all reasonably practicable steps to keep the Site open and available;

33.3 The Trade Contractor shall take all reasonably practicable steps to continue with the Trade Contract Works.

34. SETTLEMENT OF DISPUTES
Clause 36 of the *D&M Contract* shall apply also to this Trade Contract as if set out in full but with such consequential amendments as are necessary. The Adjudicator shall be the person so named or appointed under the D&M Contract, whose terms of engagement may be supplemented by any further terms agreed between the [Employer/D&M Contractor] and the Trade Contractor and incorporated into his appointment.

35. GOVERNING LAW
This Trade Contact shall be governed by English law, and the parties submit to the jurisdiction of the English Courts.

CONTENTS OF THE PROPOSED PRO FORMA TRADE CONTRACT
RECITALS
Alternative I – Where the Trade Contractor is employed initially by the Employer
Alternative II – Where the Trade Contractor is employed initially by the D&M Contractor

CLAUSES
1   Definitions and interpretation
2   Scope of Trade Contract, Novation and Warranty Agreements
        Alternative I
        Alternative II
3   Application of the D&M Contract
4   Trade Contractor's obligations
5   Instructions and drawings
6   Statutory Requirements
7   Other Project Works

[A copy of the full contract is available upon application to Trench Farrow and Partners, 32 Chapter St, Westminster, London SW1. Telephone 071-931 7688]

Appendix 4: Duties of design consultants

PRECONSTRUCTION STAGE

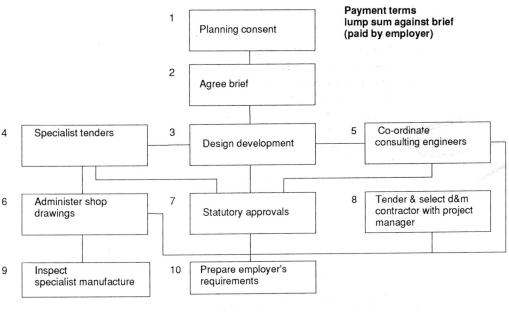

Payment terms
lump sum against brief
(paid by employer)

1 Planning consent

2 Agree brief

4 Specialist tenders

3 Design development

5 Co-ordinate consulting engineers

6 Administer shop drawings

7 Statutory approvals

8 Tender & select d&m contractor with project manager

9 Inspect specialist manufacture

10 Prepare employer's requirements

d&m contractor agree target cost

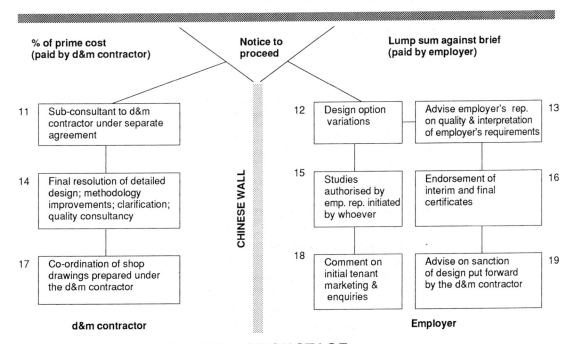

% of prime cost
(paid by d&m contractor)

Notice to proceed

Lump sum against brief
(paid by employer)

11 Sub-consultant to d&m contractor under separate agreement

12 Design option variations

13 Advise employer's rep. on quality & interpretation of employer's requirements

14 Final resolution of detailed design; methodology improvements; clarification; quality consultancy

15 Studies authorised by emp. rep. initiated by whoever

16 Endorsement of interim and final certificates

17 Co-ordination of shop drawings prepared under the d&m contractor

18 Comment on initial tenant marketing & enquiries

19 Advise on sanction of design put forward by the d&m contractor

CHINESE WALL

d&m contractor

Employer

CONSTRUCTION STAGE

Figure 12: Architect and design leader – division of principal duties under employer and d&m contractor agreements

PRECONSTRUCTION STAGE

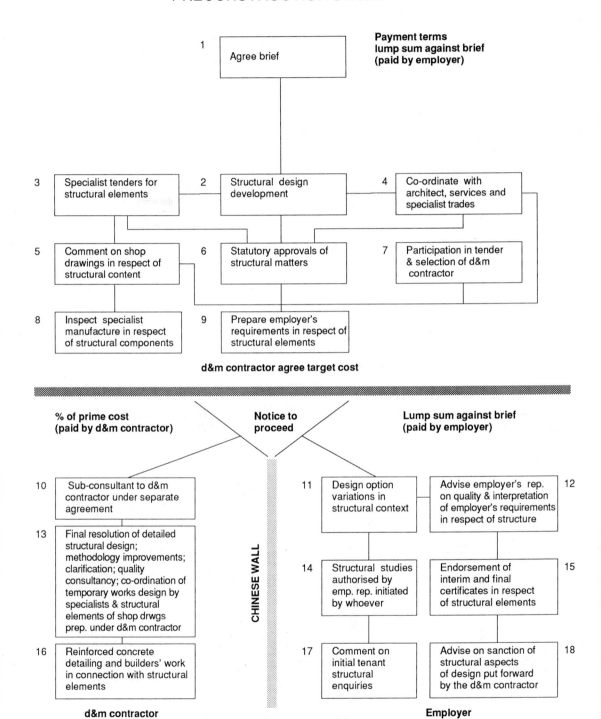

Figure 13: Structural engineer – division of principal duties under employer and d&m contractor agreements

PRECONSTRUCTION STAGE

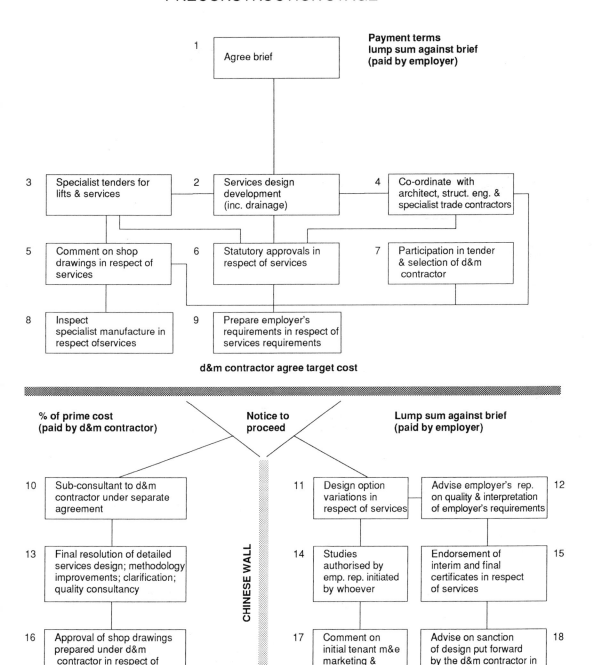

1 Agree brief

**Payment terms
lump sum against brief
(paid by employer)**

3 Specialist tenders for lifts & services

2 Services design development (inc. drainage)

4 Co-ordinate with architect, struct. eng. & specialist trade contractors

5 Comment on shop drawings in respect of services

6 Statutory approvals in respect of services

7 Participation in tender & selection of d&m contractor

8 Inspect specialist manufacture in respect of services

9 Prepare employer's requirements in respect of services requirements

d&m contractor agree target cost

**% of prime cost
(paid by d&m contractor)**

**Notice to
proceed**

**Lump sum against brief
(paid by employer)**

10 Sub-consultant to d&m contractor under separate agreement

11 Design option variations in respect of services

12 Advise employer's rep. on quality & interpretation of employer's requirements

13 Final resolution of detailed services design; methodology improvements; clarification; quality consultancy

CHINESE WALL

14 Studies authorised by emp. rep. initiated by whoever

15 Endorsement of interim and final certificates in respect of services

16 Approval of shop drawings prepared under d&m contractor in respect of services

17 Comment on initial tenant m&e marketing & enquiries

18 Advise on sanction of design put forward by the d&m contractor in respect of services

d&m contractor

Employer

CONSTRUCTION STAGE

Figure 14: Services consultant – division of principal duties under employer and d&m contractor agreements (assuming a series of m&e trade packages with design in construction stage co-ordinated by the consultant)